THE BOOK OF KNOWLEDGE
FROM THE MISHNAH TORAH OF MAIMONIDES

Royal College of Physicians of Edinburgh
Publication No. 55

Printed in Great Britain by
Geo. Stewart & Co. Ltd., Meadowbank Works
67 Marionville Road, Edinburgh

Typesetting and Design by
SET
4 Cambusnethan Street, Edinburgh

August 1981

THE BOOK
OF
KNOWLEDGE

from the
Mishnah Torah
of Maimonides

Translated from the Hebrew

by

H. M. Russell and Rabbi J. Weinberg

THE ROYAL COLLEGE OF PHYSICIANS OF
EDINBURGH
1981

CONTENTS

	Page
Foreword	i
Introduction	iii
Glossary and Explanatory Terms	ix
Treatise 1: The Foundation of the Torah	1
Treatise 2: Discernment	28
Treatise 3: The Study of the Torah	50
Treatise 4: Idolatry	70
Treatise 5: Repentance	109

FOREWORD

Maimonides was a great philosopher-physician whose writings are concerned with the nature of the relations of man to the Creator of the universe and also with the practical problems of everyday life, especially those of health and disease. He appears as essentially a practical man seeking to provide guidance for a way of life that allows both the soul and body of man to overcome the difficulties that beset him in this world. Today, he is little known except to scholars and to philosophers. The College therefore is glad to have an opportunity to publish a new translation of part of one of his major works.

Dr. Helen Russell has a long association with the College having become a member in 1925 and a Fellow in 1929. In 1970 she gave the College a sum of money to endow the J. W. Ballantyne Prize for work on the inheritance of disease. She decided to study Hebrew when she retired from her work as pathologist to the Christie Hospital in Manchester and returned to her home town. Her teacher has been Dr. J. Weinberg, BA, PhD, now Rabbi Emeritus of the Edinburgh Hebrew Congregation, who has helped her with the translation and checked carefully the final manuscript. The College wishes to thank Dr. Russell and Dr. Weinberg for introducing to many of us for the first time the writings of one of the foremost scholars of all time, and we think that others will appreciate their labour of love.

J. A. Strong
President

INTRODUCTION

Maimonides (1135–1204 CE) is the name by which English-speaking scholars generally know the Jewish physician philosopher Rabbi Moshe ben Maimon; from the initial letters of these names he is called by the Jews RaMBaM. His family was said to have been descended from Judah the Patriach who compiled the first Mishnah in the first century of this era.

He was born in Cordova, the beautiful Spanish city on the Guadalquivir, famous for its learning, and buildings and gardens. As his father, a distinguished scholar, gave him early instruction, one may assume that he was well grounded in Arabic and Hebrew, and he later devoted himself to the study of Greek Medicine and Theology. He was familiar with the works of Hippocrates and Galen and was a keen follower of Aristotle's teaching on the importance of observing nature and natural phenomena carefully. He must have been familiar with the Medical Canon of Avicenna (980–1037 CE) and he was a pupil of Averröes (1126–1198 CE) in Cordova. These two Islamic philosopher-scientists both practiced as physicians and wrote treatises on medicine which have been widely read.

He and his family became refugees in a fanatical Moorish Moslem invasion which destroyed much of Cordova, and after wandering for some years in North Africa he settled in Cairo and became physician to Saladin and his entourage. From Cairo he visited Palestine, which was in Christian hands at that time, and when he died his body was brought to Tiberias: his grave there is an important monument in that city to this day. It may be of interest to some readers that the figure of the Hakim in The Talisman by Sir Walter Scott may reflect something of the medical world in Cairo in which Maimonides held a prominent place while he served Saladin as physician to his family and court.

In Jewish learning he has been placed second to Moses as a law-giver who brought order into the almost boundless collections of Hebrew tradition and discussion which lie scattered in the Midrash, Mishnah, Gemara and other Talmudic writings.

He has also been described as the founder of rational scriptural exegesis seeking to explain the Bible in the light of reason, accepting allegorical explanations in some texts and the limits of human understanding in others. He showed that laws which might seem meaningless were important if one studied the ancient customs of the Chaldean idolaters, and that there were sensible and excellent reasons for their introduction given the human situation to which they referred.

He could also be called a reconciler, blending the past with the present, showing how essential it had been for Israel to keep apart from idolatrous neighbours and their infamous practices. He knew that people cannot change their customs suddenly, but that they must be weaned from them by something similar but different and better. It was not the worship of the sun and moon and stars which was so inimical to Israelite belief, but the abominable practices which accompanied it, such as throwing children into the fire, temple prostitution, and orgies which were associated with human sacrifice. Sacrifice was universal in the ancient world and it was better 'under strict rules to sacrifice a lamb or a dove rather than children'.[1]

He was said to have been of a gentle and philosophic disposition, but in his life as a physician he realised that understanding comes and is advanced by performing the duty — by being absorbed in the actual event rather than by meditation. His experience and careful observations allowed him to appreciate the reasonableness of laws about food and drink and cleanliness, about personal hygiene and human relationships, and those dealing with the management of domestic animals.

He never claimed omniscience or to know what he did not understand; he rejected what did not appeal to human reason in the teaching of his predecessors, and recognised and accepted the limits of human knowledge of his day. He was well aware of the interplay of psychic and somatic factors in disease which seems to have been little thought of by his contemporaries,[2] and he appreciated that intelligence

[1] Epstein, I. *Judaism* 1959 London: Penguin
[2] Moses Maimonides. *Anglo-Jewish papers in connection with the eighth centenary of his birth*, 1935. Socino Press, London. Edited by Dr. I. Epstein. In this W. M. Feldman quotes a tribute of a Moslem contemporary poet to Maimonides, the first six lines of which are:
'Contrast Maimon's with great Galen's art,
Health to the body Galen can impart,
But the wise Hebrew with a two-fold skill
Relieves both mind and body of its ill!
Shows how base ignorance can hurt the soul
While wisdom counteracting makes it whole.'

and co-operation in a patient could contribute to successful treatment. In his treatise on asthma he advised his royal patient to study for himself where, and how, he could live most comfortably.

Maimonides lived at a time of great material and intellectual turbulence in the countries surrounding the Mediterranean: people were scattered by wars, piracy and persecution, and by famines and epidemics of disease. The Crusades were being fought, the Waldenses arose, and the beginnings of the Renaissance encouraged the dreams of alchemists and mystics and the writers of Romance and Chivalry.

It was in these circumstances that he decided to write a short recapitulation of the written Law and the oral traditions of Israel, a Mishnah Torah, for the scattered Jewish communities, some of whom had taken refuge in remote islands. This state of affairs among the Jewish people was in some ways a repetition of what had happened to Israel more than a thousand years earlier after the destruction of the second Temple by the Romans in 70 CE when the remains of the Jewish tribes were scattered to the ends of the known world and sold as slaves. It was at that time that Judah the Patriach realised that the traditions and oral Law of Israel were about to be lost and he set up a school to write down all that was known or could be remembered in his Mishnah. This great work, which was not completed until 189 CE by his pupils, saved Judaism and was the basis of judgements and discussions which are contained in the *Gemara* which was completed about 500 CE. The Mishnah and *Gemara* form the basis of Talmudic literature which was not published completely for centuries after that date. In the introduction to his Mishnah Maimonides justifies his new review of the teaching of the Law because eleven centuries and eight years has passed since the Mishnah of Rabbi Judah the Patriach had been completed.

This 12th century Mishnah Torah of Maimonides consists of eighty three short treatises contained in fourteen books which cover briefly the Laws, customs, traditions and knowledge of Israel to which the author added his own more modern insight and knowledge. It was immediately accepted by his own people. His other famous work, the *Moreh Nebuchim* (a Guide for the perplexed), was written in Arabic for a favourite pupil and was too unorthodox when it appeared, but later it was translated into Latin and became a textbook in the European schools of learning, and must have had a signal influence on the course of the reformation of thought which was spreading slowly in Europe. His treatises on medical subjects were mostly written in Arabic.

In the evolution of scholarship in Europe in this era it was natural that Greek and Latin, the languages of the then great powers, were learned. Israel was a very small people, but it is regrettable that Hebrew, which has a literature stretching from the Pentateuch to the Nobel Prizewinner J. S. Agnon, has been neglected even by those who claim to teach the Bible. Perhaps that neglect is now passing and the treasuries of Jewish literature will be studied afresh by those who are interested in the development of the human psyche.

It appears that the Jewish people were ahead of others in the development of consciousness and the use of reason at a time when the human psyche was functioning at an instinctive emotional level. Rather early in history they appreciated the reality and significance of what was good or evil for human survival and were not unduly optimistic. They did not separate sacred from profane, but held that all life and the unfolding of history were sacred. They equated wisdom and the search for knowledge with piety, believing that study and the pursuit of knowledge about the world helped one to fulfil the first commandment. The wise and learned became thus the aristocracy in Israel and they looked to a future (Messianic) happiness for mankind and strove for it, instead of dreaming about a golden age of past childhood.

The age-old wisdom of Israel combined with the 12th century medical philosophy of Maimonides seems very relevant to the individual and world problems of today. Its discipline is like that of a strict religious order to a Protestant, yet one in which it is a duty to enjoy life as fully as possible while aiming at moderation in all its aspects. A doctor notes especially the emphasis laid on cleanliness which was linked with a strict discipline of life and near to the idea of holiness; the importance of a whole and properly functioning body and the discipline required for its maintenance; and that the decency and dignity which raise mankind above animal inclinations were never allowed to be forgotten.

It is not likely that a 20th century physician can understand the thought of the 12th century or appreciate the conditions of life at that date; but, the advances which have been made in medicine during the last hundred years, and the medical records which have been collected from many parts of the underdeveloped world, allow one to grasp why Maimonides seems to have concentrated his advice to his people on preventive rather than curative medicine, on the maintenance of a sound body by such means as were available then.

In the Mediterranean countries in the Middle Ages

probably half the population died in early childhood and many more before adolescence. Few would survive to the age of forty or sixty years, which C. G. Jung considered the decades in which an individual might reach psychological maturity. The epidemics of plague and other infectious diseases which spread periodically along the Mediterranean littoral were accepted like other calamities of nature such as earthquakes, and there was no escape from them except by flight, or special wisdom or good fortune. The endemic diseases such as malaria and schistosomiasis (which is still the scourge of the Nile valley) were not understood until many decades after microscopes became generally available in the middle of the 19th century.

Perhaps, therefore, it may be surmised that Maimonides, with insight, common sense and humility, taught his people what they might do to preserve health using long tried beliefs, customs and disciplines which had enabled some of them to say that it had been 'well with them', that they had 'prolonged their days'.

Note on the Translation

Some apology may be needed for offering translations of treatises of Maimonides' Mishnah Torah to colleagues. His works have been translated into many languages, both by scholars and scribes, and the difficulties must have been great and very various. Translation from Hebrew into English is beset with problems, indeed a close translation is hardly readable because Hebrew is a very brief, concise and vivid language. The first sentence of the 23rd Psalm in English uses nine words but in Hebrew only four are needed. Biblical Hebrew has no true subordinate clauses, uses two genders, simple verbs and many prefixes and suffixes. Short sentences are strung together in chains with conjunctions, the common-est of which is *and,* and the syntax resembles that of con-versation rather than composition, which is perhaps related to its old oral tradition. Translation into easily read English therefore requires very free handling of a text and the danger of mistranslation or losing an exact meaning is great; each re-reading of a text may suggest a new arrangement of English syntax and the use of different words. Needless to say, it is impossible to convey the 'spice of idiom' or the punning of Hebrew in English. In addition to that there seems to be a deliberate ambiguity in some of the writings as if the author were saying 'Choose thou', or 'Your guess may be as good as mine'. There is also the possibility that a scribe copying a mediaeval script before the days of printing may have made a mistake; an apparently trivial error can change the meaning of a whole sentence in Hebrew.

GLOSSARY

Amida
Standing up and reciting the prescribed Eighteen Blessings.

Asherah
A grove or a tree worshipped by the heathens.

Beth Din
The Jewish court of Law.

Commandment
This word was sometimes restricted to the ten commandements revealed to Moses on Mount Sinai, but there were many others, 613 in all. Of these, 248 were positive and 365 negative commands. Tradition taught that the negative commands were concerned with 'the fear of the Lord' and the positive with the 'love of the Lord'. Some were no longer applicable after the destruction of the Temple, others only applied in Israel.

Deoth
Discernment. The meaning indicated in Proverbs 9:10, 'The fear of the Lord is the beginning of wisdom: and knowledge (Deoth) of the holy is understanding'.

Gehenna
The valley of the Hinnom south-west of Jerusalem where at one time idolaters sacrificed children to Moloch. It became a general rubbish heap and midden for the city. Parts of it were burning continually and clouds of smoks and insects hung over it. It meant a place of complete destruction.

Genizah
A hiding place or store in which all worn-out religious manuscripts were placed.

Ishim
In Hebrew there were ten names for man and in the time of Maimonides, the highest may have been *Enosh;* it indicated the highest degree of human being who might be in touch with the *Ishim* who were the lowest of messengers (see chapter 2, paragraph 7). No child, mentally defective person or criminal could attain this degree.

Karet
The punishment of cutting off, either at the hands of God or through expulsion from the people.

Malach	Any messenger, as in Malachi, My messenger; translated into European languages as angel.
Messiah	Noun from the verb *mashach,* to anoint. Perhaps easily mixed up with *Moshia* (Saviour).
Mezuzah	A small case fixed to the lintels of the door of a house, containing parchment on which the texts are inscribed.
Midrash	The interpretation of Scripture.
Mishnah	The repetition of the Law. The first *Mishnah* was the collection of all the written and oral Law of Israel and was written after the destruction of the second temple at the sack of Jerusalem by the Romans.
Mitzvah	A positive command. A precept which gives pleasure to the doer as well as merit; insight and judgment increasing as the deed is performed.
Nisan	A lunar month between March and April.
Olam-ha-ba	Translated as the world to come. It is a Jewish theological term. Sometimes it can be interpreted as a personal hope of individual reward in the hereafter or heaven. It may also refer to a future Messianic era when righteousness and justice rule in this world.
Orlah	Literally foreskin or uncircumcision. The use of the fruit of a tree was forbidden until it was three years old, as being the fruit of uncircumcision.
Pardes	Literally garden or paradise. It is said to be of Persian origin and means the orchard of delight, not the garden of Eden. It came to mean the realm of mystical and metaphysical speculation.
Pentateuch	The first five books of the Old Testament. These were considered to have been divinely inspired and not a jot or tittle of it was allowed to be altered. Ancient scrolls were handwritten by trained scribes and no copy with even the smallest error was preserved.
Punishments	There were no prisons in ancient Israel. Punishments were stripes of an appointed

	number, ostracism and excommunication. Capital punishment was by stoning, burning, beheading and hanging.
Rabbi	A teacher and master.
Servant	There was no slavery in Israel, but a man might bind himself to serve another for a term of years for various reasons, such as poverty, or to repay a debt or to compensate for a crime. The servant's time was at his master's disposal, not his body as in slavery.
Shechinah	The indwelling Spirit of the Lord, the Divine Presence.
Shield of David	A six-pointed star.
Tephillim	Phylacteries in Greek. Two leather straps that an orthodox Jew binds round his left arm and head at the hour of prayer, in compliance with the command, 'Thou shalt bind them for a sign upon thine hand and for frontlets between thine eyes' (Deuteronomy 6: 4-9; 11:18-21). A small box attached to the straps contains a parchment on which the texts are inscribed in minute writing.
Tishri	A lunar month between September and October.
Tohorot	Purity. It is usually translated into English as 'cleanliness' which is inadequate, as the word implies many things including permitted marital relations, personal and communal hygiene.
Torah	The teaching of the Law. It usually refers to the Pentateuch. Later Torah became synonymous with wider learning and the study of the application of the Law to changing circumstances.
Transgression	Violation of a negative command; repentance was remorse for this violation.

ACKNOWLEDGEMENTS

We wish to thank the late Dr Alister Alexander who first suggested that this translation of part of the writings of Maimonides would be of interest to Fellows and Members of the College. We are indebted to Miss D. McKay a former member of the staff of the College Library who undertook the work of retyping the various drafts of this translation and who carefully checked the Biblical references in the Authorised Version of the Old Testament. We also wish to thank Dr R. Passmore for help in the editing and final preparation.

Treatise 1
THE FOUNDATION OF THE TORAH

The Laws concerning the foundations of the Torah are six positive and four negative, namely:

1. To know that there is a God.
2. Not to support that there is another.
3. To believe in His unity.
4. To love Him.
5. To fear Him.
6. To hallow His name.
7. Not to profane His name.
8. Not to destroy anything which bears His name.
9. To listen to a prophet who speaks in His name.
10. Not to test (tempt) Him.

The explanation of these commandments is given in the following chapters of Treatise 1.

Chapter 1

1. The very foundation and firm support of all wisdom is to know that there is a primary reality which caused all to be; and that all that exists in heaven and earth and all between heaven and eath could not exist without the truth of this reality.
2. If He were not, nothing could have been called into existence.
3. On the other hand, if all other beings did not exist, He would remain; for His existence does not depend on theirs. He would not cease if they ceased — blessed be He! He is not dependent upon one of them. So the reality of His being is not comparable to the reality of any other existing thing.
4. This is what the prophet said, 'the Lord is the true God', (Jeremiah 10:10),[1] and the Torah states: 'there is no one like unto Him', implying that He alone is the Truth and there is no other Truth like His Truth (Deuteronomy 4:39).
5. This reality is God of the universe and Lord of all the

---

[1] It was a strict duty in Judaism always to acknowledge the source of information or instruction and the greatest care was given to supplying references from the Scriptures.

earth. He guides the celestial spheres[1] with a might which is complete and unceasing, for the sphere turns continually which it could not do without a cause. The Blessed One turns it although He has no body or hand.

6. To understand this is the positive commandment which states: 'I am the Lord thy God' (Exodus 20:2). Anyone who believes that there is another god violates the negative commandment which says: 'Thou shalt have no other gods before me' (Exodus 20:3) for he denies the very principle upon which all depends.

7. God is one, neither two nor more, but a unity, unlike other unities in the universe which may have many parts or like a body which is divided into parts. So the unity of God is quite different from anything else in the world. If there were many deities it would mean that they had body and form because individuals only differ from one another in bodily form. If the Creator had a body and form He would have an end, a ceasing. It is impossible to imagine a body that does not end and whose strength does not wane. Our God — blessed be He! — has strength to which there is no end and does not falter because the sphere continues to revolve for ever by His force which is not a bodily force. Because He is incorporeal, none of the happenings which occur to parts of a body can be attributed to Him, so it is impossible that He should be but one. The understanding of monotheism is a positive commandment (Deuteronomy 6:4).

8. The Torah and the prophesies proclaim that the Holy One has no bodily form, for it is said: 'He is Lord in heaven above and in earth beneath' (Deuteronomy 4:39) and a body cannot be in two places at once. Further on Sinai no bodily form was seen (Deuteronomy 4:15) and Isaiah said: 'To whom then will ye liken me, or shall I be equal?' (Isaiah 40: 25).

9. This being so, why were there allusions in the writings of the Torah to 'under His feet' (Exodus 24:10); 'written with the finger of God' (Exodus 31:18); 'the hand of the Lord' (Exodus 9:3); 'the eyes of the Lord' (Deuteronomy 11:12); 'the ears of the Lord' (Numbers 11:18); and such like? All these expressions are related to the capacity of men who only understand material things, and the Torah spoke the language that men could understand. These sayings are all metaphorical. When it is said: 'If I whet my glittering sword'

[1] Here and elsewhere in the treatise the view of the universe is pre-Copernican.

(Deuteronomy 32:41), has He a sword and does He kill? All is allegorical. Elsewhere a prophet said that he saw the Holy One and that His 'garment was white as snow' (Daniel 7:9); and another saw Him with dyed garments of Bozrah, (Isaiah 63:1). At the Red Sea, Moses our teacher saw the Lord as a 'man of war' engaged in battle (Exodus 15:3); and upon Sinai clothed as a reader of the congregation (Exodus 19:19), meaning that He has no likeness or form. All these expressions are images and visions of the prophets. The truth is that the mind of man is not able to understand nor is he able to penetrate here, as the verse states: 'Canst thou by searching find out the Almighty unto perfection?' (Job 11:7).

10. What did Moses our teacher want to understand when he asked: 'I beseech thee, shew me thy glory' (Exodus 33: 18)? He sought to know in his heart the reality of the existence of the Holy One — blessed be He! — in the same way as he recognised individual persons whose appearance was engraved on his heart and distinguished from all others. So Moses our teacher wished to see in his mind the Holy One separated from all other creatures until he understood His reality as it is. The Blessed One answered that it is not in the power of living man, compounded of body and soul, to grasp that reality in its perfection. But the Holy One did make known to Moses what no one has known before or since; and he grasped the truth of a reality which was different from all other things, in the same way as one can recognise by body and clothes someone whom one sees from behind and can recognise as different from other men. The verse which suggests this states: 'and thou shalt see my back parts:[1] but my face shall not be seen' (Exodus 33:23).

11. Since it is clear that the Holy One has neither body nor form, it is also clear that nothing that happens to bodies can happen to Him, no joining or dividing, no position or measure, no ascent or descent, no right or left, no front or back, no sitting or standing. As He is not influenced by time, He has no beginning or end or any measure in years, nor does He change for there is nothing changeable in Him. There is no death or life in Him as in living bodies; no folly or wisdom such as are found in man. He neither sleeps nor wakens, is neither angry nor laughs, does not rejoice or grieve, has no silence or speech like the speech of man. The sages said also

[1]Behind or back may imply the past history of Israel (Jewish homily).

that in Heaven there was no sitting, no standing, no competition or weariness.

12. Because of this all the descriptions of the Holy One in the Torah, and those uttered by the prophets, are merely metaphorical and figurative. For example, it states: 'He that sitteth in the heavens shall laugh' (Psalm 2:4), 'they have provoked me to anger' (Deutronomy 32:21), 'the Lord rejoiced' (Deutronomy 28:63) and the like. The sages said that the Torah is written in the speech of ordinary men. It is also written, 'do they provoke me to anger?' (Jeremiah 7: 19), and 'I am the Lord, I change not' (Malachi 3:6). If the Holy One was sometimes angry and sometimes mirthful, he would be subject to change for such attributes are only found in dark and lowly bodies dwelling in houses of clay, made of dust. But the Holy One — blessed be He! — is exalted above all that.

Chapter 2

1. It is a positive commandment to love this great and awe-inspiring God and also to fear Him, as the verse states: 'thou shalt love the Lord thy God' (Deuteronomy 6:5), and 'thou shalt fear the Lord thy God' (Deuteronomy 6:13).

2. But how does one learn to love and fear Him? When man contemplates God's works and His great and marvellous creatures (by thorough study), he sees from them wisdom that is without estimate or end, and is immediately filled with love and praise and longs ardently to know the Holy Name even as David said, 'my soul thirsteth for God' (Psalm 42:2). And when a man thinks about these mighty matters he draws back and trembles and realises that he is a minute creature, lowly and dark, capable only of a little knowledge in the presence of perfect knowledge, as David said 'When I consider thy heavens ... what is man, that thou art mindful of him? and the son of man, that thou visiteth him?' (Psalm 8:3-4). In accordance with these sayings I explain great principles from the works of the Lord of the universe so that there may be an opening for one who wants to understand to love God. About such love the sages said that by it one comes to know who spoke and how the universe came into existence.

3. All that the Blessed One created in the world He divided into three parts. Some are composite creatures of matter and shape which exist and pass away like the bodies of men, animals, plants and minerals. Some are composite creations

of matter and shape which do not change in shape and form like the first group; their form is fixed for ever and their substance is unchanging. They are the planets and the stars around them; their matter is not like other matter nor is their form like other forms. Others are creations which have form but no matter and they are messengers who have no body or substance but they differ from one another.

4.   What did the prophets mean when they said that they saw a fiery, winged messenger? That is prophetic, enigmatic vision, a way of saying that a thing has no body or weight, as when it was said: 'For the Lord thy God is a consuming fire' (Deuteronomy 4:24). That is a figure of speech and a further example is: 'Who maketh his angels spirits, his ministers a flaming fire' (Psalm 104:4).

5.   How are messengers separated from one another if they have no bodies? They are not alike in their essence and each is lower than another and derives its power from the one above, and all derive their power from the Holy One — blessed be He — and from His excellence. As Solomon in his wisdom said: 'for he that is higher than the highest regardeth' (Ecclesiastes 5:8).

6.   When we say that one is lower than the other, it is not lower in position, like a man who sits lower than his friend, but like two wise men, one of whom is wiser than the other and so excels him, just as a master craftsman is superior to his workmen.

7.   The difference in the names of the messengers depends upon their degree and for this reason they are called holy *chayot* (beings) of the Most High who is above all. They are called *ophnanim, erellam, hashmalin, seraphim,* messengers, gods, *cherubim* and *ishim* (see glossary). These names of the messengers indicate their ten degrees and there is nothing higher than them except God — blessed be He! They are the degrees of what are called *chayot* and the prophets spoke of them as being under the the throne of glory. The tenth degree *ishim* are the messengers who talk to the prophets and are seen by them in prophetic visions. they are called *ishim* because their degree is near to the degree of man's intelligence.

8.   These messengers exist and recognise the Creator and know Him intimately according to their degree, not their size. Even those of highest degree are unable to understand the reality of the Creator as He truly is. Their intelligence cannot attain that, although it reaches further than that of the lower degrees. Thus, each above the other to the tenth

understands the Creator in a way that man, joined of matter
and form, cannot attain. And none can understand the
Creator as he understands Himself.

9. All that exists, except the Creator, from the first form
to the smallest moth, which might be in the centre of the
earth, exist by the power of His reality. He knows Himself
and His own might, majesty and reality. He knows all,
nothing is hidden from Him.

10. The Holy One recognises His own verity and knows it as
it really is, and does not know it with an intelligence outside
Himself as we do; for we and our intelligence are not one.
But the Blessed Creator, He and His understanding and existence are one, in every aspect of His unity. If this were not
so, He would live apart from His intelligence and there would
then be several gods — He, His existence and His intelligence.
It is not so. He is unity in every aspect. You must say that
He is the knowledge and the knower and intelligence itself
all in one. The mouth has no power to describe this nor the
ear to perceive this, nor can the heart of man understand this
perfection. Thus one speaks of 'the life of Pharaoh' (Genesis
42:15,16) or the 'life of thy soul' (I Samuel 1:26) but not
'the life of God'. One says 'the living God' (Judges 8:19). The
Creator and his life are not two as is the life of messengers.
Therefore He does not recognise created things or know them
as we creatures do, but He knows them as He knows Himself.
Thus He knows all and all depends on His existence.

11. The matters which we have spoken of in these two
chapters are merely a drop in the ocean of what ought to be
explained. These deep matters are expounded in the symbolic
vision, known as the chariot (Ezekiel 1:1-28).

12. The sages commanded us not to give instruction on
these matters except to an individual of wisdom and intelligence. Then the headings of the chapters might be given to
help him to understand a small fraction of the matter, and
his own intelligence would probe its depth in the end. These
matters are very profound and not all intelligences can grasp
them. Solomon, in his wisdom, said concerning them metaphorically: 'The lambs[1] are for thy clothing' (Proverbs 27:
26) meaning 'they are for thee alone, do not spread them
abroad to all'. He said also: 'Let them be only thine own, and
not strangers, with thee (Proverbs 5:17) and he said 'Honey

---

[1] In Hebrew this is a pun on the words lamb and secret.

and milk are under thy tongue' (Song of Songs 4:11). The early sages said this meant that these matters should remain unspoken.[1]

Chapter 3

1.   The celestial spheres are called heaven, firmament, abode of the Lord, nebulae, and there are nine of them. The nearest to us is the moon's sphere and the next one is the sphere of stars wherein is Mercury. The third sphere contains Venus and the fourth above us contains the sun. In the fifth sphere is Mars. In the sixth is judgment (Jupiter). The seventh sphere has Saturn. All the other stars which we see in the heavens are in the eighth sphere. The ninth sphere is that which turns every day from east to west and encloses and surrounds all the others. You see all the stars as if they were in one sphere, although they are set one above the other, because the spheres are clear and as transparent as glass and sapphire, and stars in the eighth sphere may appear to be lower than the first sphere.

2.   Each of the eight spheres wherein are the stars are divided into many spheres, one above the other, and are like the layers of an onion. Some of them go round from west to east and some from east to west like the ninth sphere. Between them there is no space.

3.   The spheres are neither light nor heavy, they are not red or black, nor any other colour. What we see as blue is an illusion due to the height of the atmosphere. They have also no taste or odour, for they do not have the characteristics of the bodies which are found below them.

4.   All these spheres encircle the world like a globe and the earth hangs in the centre. A few stars are attached to small spheres that do not encircle the earth; they are small spheres not attached to the large ones.

5.   Eighteen spheres surround the universe and there are eight small spheres which do not surround the universe. From the journey of the stars and the distance they travel each day and hour, and their movement south to north and from north to south, and their distance above the earth, from all these the number of the spheres and their circles are known. This is the science of the spheres and planets about which the Greeks have written many books.

[1] The Rabbis forbad discussion or preaching about the vision of Ezekiel.

6.   The ninth sphere which encircles them all was divided by the ancient sages into twelve parts and to each part the name was given of an image which you see in the stars below them and is fixed under them. They are the Zodiac — the Ram, the Bull, the Twins, the Crab, the Lion, the Virgin, the Scales, the Scorpion, the Archer, the Goat, the Water Carrier and the Fishes.

7.   The ninth sphere itself has no division or resemblance to any of these, and it has no stars. But by joining the stars of the eight spheres, it is possible to see with the big stars a pattern of forms somewhat like them (the Zodiac). The twelve were not fixed opposite the twelve parts except at the time of the Flood when their names were given to them, but in the present day they have moved a little because all the stars in the eighth sphere move round like the sun and moon but revolve slowly. The sun and moon revolve in one day a distance which takes all the stars about seventy years.

8.   Among all the visible stars there are some smaller than the earth and some are many times larger. The earth is about 40 times bigger than the moon and the sun is a hundred and seventy times bigger than the earth. So the moon is a 6,800th part of the sun. There is no star bigger than the sun and none smaller than those of the second sphere.

9.   All the stars and spheres have souls, intelligence and understanding. They exist and recognise Him who spoke and the universe came into being. Every one according to its size and degree glorifies and extols the Creator, as do the messengers. And just as they recognise the Holy One, they also recognise themselves and the messengers above them. But the intelligence of the stars and the spheres is less than that of the messengers, but is greater than the intelligence of the sons of man.

10.   Below the moon's sphere the Lord created a substance different from that of the celestial spheres. He created four elements of this substance that were not like the forms of the spheres, and each of these elements was part of the substance. The first element is fire which when joined with part of the substance issues as fire. The second element is air which when joined with some of the substance issues as air. The third element is water and the fourth element is earth. So, under the firmament there are four elements, one above the other, encircling one another around like a sphere. The first element, which is near the moon's sphere, is fire, below it is air, below the air is the water and below the water is the earth, and there is no unfilled space between them.

11. These four elements have no soul; they have no intelligence or understanding but are as dead matter. Each one behaves in a way which it does not understand and cannot change. Of these David said: 'Praise the Lord from the earth, ye dragons, and all deeps: Fire, and hail; snow, and vapours; stormy wind fulfilling his word' (Psalm 148:7-8). These words mean: Sons of men praise Him in his might that you see in fire, and hail, and the other creations that you see below the firmament. Their might is ever manifest to both small and great.

Chapter 4

1. The four elements — fire, air, water and earth — are the foundation of all that is created below the firmament, all humans, animals, birds, creeping things and fishes, all plants, metals, precious stones and pearls, and other stones for building, and which form mountains and thick dust; all these are mixtures of the four elements. Thus we find that all bodies below the firmament — except the four elements — are a union of substance and form made up of the four, while the four elements themselves are not composite.

2. Fire and air have the tendency to go upwards from the centre of the earth towards the firmament, and water and earth to go downwards towards the centre which is the lowest place of all; and their movement is not due to intelligence or desire, but is a fixed property of their natures. The nature of fire is hot and dry and lighter than all; air is warm and moist, water is cool and moist, earth is dry and cool and heavier than them all. Water is lighter than earth, so it is found above the earth. Air is lighter than water, so it hovers on the face of the water. Fire is lighter than air. Because these elements are the basis of all things below the firmament, it is found that every form of man and cattle and beasts, birds and fishes, and plants, and minerals, and stones are compounded of fire, air, water and dust, and the four elements are intermingled and fused so that the mixture is unlike each when it is alone. In such mixtures there is no actual fire or water, or earth or air, but all are changed into one body. All bodies formed from the four elements have coolness and heat, wet and dry combined. But there are among them bodies in which fire is strongest, as in living creatures, and they are noticeably warm; and there are some in which the earth is strongest, such as stones, and they are

9

noticeably dry. In others the element water is strong and dampness is more noticeable in them: so one warm body may be warmer than another and one may be dryer than another. Some bodies may be especially cold and some especially damp, and there are also others in which the cold and damp are noticed equally, or the hot and the dry, or heat and moisture. The action and nature of the bodies depends upon the amount of each element in the mixture.

3. And all things combined of these four elements disintegrate in the end, some within a few days, others after many years; none can escape dissolution. Even gold and ruby cannot remain but return to their elements and their return is in part to fire, in part to water and in part to air and dust.

4. Since all disintegrate into these elements, why was it said to man: 'unto dust shalt thou return'? (Genesis 3:19). Because most of him is dust. But not all which disintegrates does disolve at once into the four basic elements; it breaks down from one thing to another and in the end there is return to the elements in a circle.

5. The four elements are therefore continually and partially changing into one another day by day and hour by hour. In this manner, a part of earth near the water changes and crumbles into water and some of the water mixed with wind evaporates and becomes the air, and part of the air near fire changes and becomes fire, and fire near the air turns and changes and mixes with the air. Air, which is close to water, changes and collects and forms water, and water near the earth changes and solidifies and becomes solid earth. But the change is very slow in the passage of time and does not go on until all water is air, or all air is fire, for it is impossible for any one of the four elements to be eliminated. A little fire changes into air and a little of air into fire, and so between them the changes circulate for ever.

6. This change comes from the rotation of the celestial spheres and the four elements are mixed by its rotation and they make the forms of men, living creatures, plants, vegetation, and rocks and metals. To each bit of matter God the Lord gives a form appropriate to the intelligence of *ishim* the tenth messenger, that is a shape which can be recognised by the highest intelligence of man.

7. You never see matter without form or form without matter and the heart of man with his intelligence knows that a body has both form and substance. He also knows that there are bodies whose substance contains the four elements

10

and bodies of a single disunited substance. The forms which have no substance are not seen by the eye, but the heart's eye knows them in the same way as we know the Lord of all without seeing Him with the eye.

8.   The soul of all flesh is the essence which God gave it and the special intelligence found in the soul of man is that of the perfectly intelligent man, as was written in the Torah: 'Let us make man in our image after our likeness' (Genesis 1: 26), as if to say that he should have the kind of intelligence and understanding which is without substance as do the messengers which have essence but no substance, and so resemble them. This character is not the kind which is recognised by eye, nose, mouth or cheek, or other bodily features of shape, and it is not the principle by which living things eat and drink, reproduce, feel or think, but it is the intelligence referred to in the words 'in our image and likeness'. It is spoken of many times as soul and spirit. It is necessary to be careful about these names in order than one may not err but learn what each consists of.

9.   The character of the soul *(neshamah)* is not a union of the elements that can be separated from one another and it is not the breath *(ruach)* which is essential for the body, but it is from the Lord, from Heaven. Therefore, when the body which is formed of the four elements dissolves and the breath of life which is essential to the body is lost, the soul is not destroyed. It is not needed for breath and action but has intelligence and understanding separate from matter. It knows the Creator of all and remains for ever and ever. As Solomon in his wisdom said: 'Then shall the dust return to the earth as it was and the spirit shall return unto God who gave it' (Ecclesiastes 12:7).

10.   All these matters about which we have spoken are but as a drop in a bucket. They are profound subjects but less deep than those of chapters 1 and 2. The explanation of the subjects in chapters 3 and 4 is about what is called the Work of Creation and the ancient sages advised that the subject should not be broadcast to the multitudes but to individuals by explaining and teaching.

11.   And what is the difference between the action of the chariot and the Work of Creation? The works of the chariot were not even taught to an individual unless he was a wise man gifted with intelligence. Only the chapter headings were given to him. Work of Creation was imparted to an individual although his intelligence could not understand it and he was

taught all that he could grasp about it. If so, why were they not taught to the multitude? Because every man has not the wide understanding to grasp and clarify and explain the matters perfectly.

12. When a man examines these things and recognises all creations, messengers and spheres, and man, and what happens to him, he sees the wisdom of the Holy One — blessed be He! — in all that has been formed and created. His love for the Most High grows, his soul thirsts and his flesh longs eagerly for the love of the Holy One — blessed be He! He fears and trembles with his own lowliness, poverty and smallness when he compares himself with one of the great and holy bodies and especially with one of the pure forms separated from matter which have no connection with matter at all. He finds himself as a vessel full of disgrace and reproach, empty and wanting.

13. These four chapters are concerned with commandments which the ancients related to the orchard (*pardes* — see glossary). They say four entered the orchard (Haggiagah 14b) and, although they were the great men of Israel and great scholars, not all were able to grasp these matters in their perfection. I believe that it is not fitting to walk in the orchard unless one has filled oneself with bread and meat, and that bread and meat is the knowledge of what is forbidden and what is allowed; that applies to all other commandments although they may be about small matters. According to the sages the work of the chariot is a great subject; but they said that the small subjects of life come first and are necessary to compose the mind of man and are the great good which the Holy One pours out for the tranquillity of this world. This is in order that the world to come (*Olam ha-ba* — see glossary) may be inherited and be attained by all, small and great, man and woman, whether of much or of little intelligence.

Chapter 5

1. It is a positive command to the whole house of Israel to sanctify the great and Holy Name, as was said: 'I will be hallowed among the children of Israel' (Leviticus 22:32), and they are warned not to profane the Holy Name, as the above verse states: 'Neither shall ye profane my Holy Name'.

What was to happen when an idolater forced an Israelite to transgress one of the commandments of the Torah on pain of death? He transgressed and did not suffer death because it was said of the commandments that when man performed them he must live by them and not die (Leviticus 18:5). If he is killed and did not transgress, he is guilty of his own life.

2.   To what do these words refer? To all the commandments except idolatry, immorality and bloodshed. Regarding these three, if one says 'transgress one of them or die', one must die and not transgress. And how do the words apply when the idolater purposes to benefit himself, as when he forced an Israelite to build his house or cook his meals on the Sabbath or violates a Jewish woman and the like. But if he intended only to make him violate a commandment when they were alone and not in the presence of ten Israelites, he might transgress and not die. In the presence of ten Israelites, he might not transgress but must die. This even if the idolator did not intend to make him transgress any other commandment.

3.   All these instructions apply at a time when there is no special persecution. But at a time of special edicts, as when a wicked king like Nebuchadnezzar and his associates pronounce an edict on Israel to forsake its religion or one of the commandments, he must die and not transgress any one of the commandments whether in the presence of ten Israelites or alone with the idolater.

4.   In the circumstances when a man is instructed to transgress in order to save his life and yet did not transgress but was killed, he was held responsible for his own life. And when a man was told to die and not transgress and he was killed without transgression, he thereby 'sanctified the Holy Name'. If this happens in the presence of ten Israelites, he has sanctified the Holy Name in public, like Daniel, Hananiah, Mishael, Azariah and Rabbi Akiba and his friends who were slain by the government (Rome) and who showed the highest degree of martyrdom. Of them, and of martyrdom, it was said, 'for thy sake are we killed all the day long; we are counted as sheep for the slaughter' (Psalm 44:22) and 'gather my saints together unto me; those that have made a covenant with me by sacrifice' (Psalm 50:5). And whosoever was instructed to die and not transgress and did transgress and not die 'profaned the Holy Name of God'. If this happened in the presence of ten Israelites, he profaned the name in public and violated the positive command to sanctify the Name and the negative command about profaning the Name. However, if the transgression was forced upon him, he

13

was not lashed and the *Beth Din* did not condemn him to death even for murder under duress. For neither lashes nor capital punishment were given for transgression which was not deliberate, and performed before witnesses and after due warning.[1]

Of one sacrificing his children to Moloch, it is written, 'I will set my face against that man' (Leviticus 20:5), and according to tradition, we understand that in that case there was no compulsion or mistake or ignorance. What of idolatry, which is the gravest offence of all? Idolatry under duress is not deserving of excommunication from the people or the death penalty from the *Beth Din*. In the same way all trespass against the lesser commandments is judged. Concerning immorality, it was said, 'But unto the (betrothed)[2] damsel thou shalt do nothing' (Deuteronomy 22:26). If a man can save his life and flee from the hand of a wicked king and does not do so, he is likened to the dog which returns to its vomit and he is called a wanton idolater, and is excluded from the world to come and descends to the lowest step of Gehenna (see glossary).

5. If idolaters say to women: 'Give us one of you to defile her or we will defile all', then all were to be defiled rather than that one Israelite soul be handed over. Similarly, if idolaters said to men: 'Give us one of you to be killed or we will kill all', all must be killed rather than surrender an Israelite soul. However, in circumstances when they say: 'Give us such and such a single person or we will kill all', if that person was worthy of death like Sheba, the son of Bichri (2 Samuel 20:1), he might be handed over; but they were not advised to do so at once unless he was proven guilty of a capital crime. All die rather than sacrifice a soul of Israel.

6. What was said of duress was also applied to sickness. For example, if a man was sick and near to death and the doctors said that such and such a remedy, forbidden in the Torah, might cure, they might use it. Healing might be attempted in time of danger by means forbidden in the Torah, except when these involved idolatry, immorality and murder, for even in the time of danger to life, these might not be employed in healing. If there is such transgression and recovery, the *Beth Din* inflicts due punishment.

7. Where do we learn that, even in time of danger to life,

[1] Capital punishment was therefore extremely rare, as it was almost impossible to get the witnesses necessary for a conviction.

[2] Betrothal is the important ceremony in Jewish marriage.

we do not transgress any of these three negative commands? Where it is said: 'And thou shalt love the Lord thy God with all thy heart, with all thy soul and with all thy might' (Deuteronomy 6:5), even though He takes thy life. To take the life of an Israelite to heal another soul or to save him from force is rejected by reason, and one life may not be destroyed for another. As regards immorality, it is compared with life, as was said: 'It is as if a man arose against his neighbour and slew him'. (Deuteronomy 22:26).

8. In what circumstances was it said that forbidden cures should not be used except in great danger? At a time when they gave pleasure, as for example, feeding the sick person with unclean animals and crawling animals, or giving him leaven at Passover or feeding him on the Day of Atonement. But, if there was no enjoyment, as in using plaster or a poultice of leaven at Passover, or fruit forbidden by Orlah (Leviticus 19:23), or giving drink in which the forbidden had been mixed with bitter substances not pleasant to the palate; these were allowed even when life was not in grave danger, but not mixtures of grafted fruits from the vineyard (Deuteronomy 22:9), and mixtures of meat and milk which are forbidden, even if not enjoyable. These might not be used for healing even if unpleasant, unless there is danger to life.

9. If there was a man who desired a woman and he became sick and near death and the doctors said there was no cure except that he might have her, he was to die, even if she was not wedded. Even to speak with her behind a screen was not allowed and he might die. Permission would not be given for him to speak with her behind a screen lest the daughters of Israel might become licentious and unchaste (Sanhedrin 75a).

10. Anyone who wilfully, under no duress, transgresses a commandment of the Torah and does it insolently and with a contempt profanes the Holy Name.[1] Of false swearing, it was said: 'neither shalt thou profane the name of thy God: I am the Lord' (Leviticus 19:12). If anyone profanes in the presence of ten Israelites, he has profaned the Name among many. Conversely, if a man avoids transgression and performs a commandment without special motive, and not in fear or fright, or to seek honour, but only for the sake of the Creator — blessed be He! — that man 'sanctifies the Holy Name', as Joseph the righteous did in refusing to take his master's wife.

---

[1] Profanation applies when a negative law is transgressed in public.

11. There are other matters concerned in general with profanation of the Name and these are things which anyone well versed in the Torah and renowned for righteousness may happen to do; things which his compatriots might gossip about and, although they are not transgressions, yet they profane the Name. For instance, the man who buys and does not pay the value immediately, although he has the means and the sellers demand it and he delays; or if a man is frivolous or eats and drinks among the unlettered,[1] or whose speech with his friends is not gentle and he does not welcome them kindly but is irritable and angry. In these matters it depends upon the renown of the scholar who must be very careful to examine himself and to act beyond legal requirements. If a scholar is careful in this way, speaks gently to his associates, agrees with them, receives them kindly, takes abuse without returning it, respects those who even mock him, conducts business honestly, does not spend much time with the unlettered and their gatherings, is usually seen busy with the Torah wrapped in his prayer shawl and wearing his phylacteries, and does all that is required of the Law without going to extremes or isolating himself, then all will praise and love him and desire to follow his ways. Such a man sanctifies the Lord and of him the verse says: 'Thou art My servant, O Israel, in whom I will be glorified' (Isaiah 49:3).

Chapter 6

1. The Torah requires punishment by flogging for anyone who destroys one of the Holy and perfect Names by which the Holy One — blessed be He! — is known, for it is said of idolatry: 'Ye shall ... destroy the names of them out of that place. Ye shall not do so to the Lord your God' (Deuteronomy 12:3-4).
2. There are seven such Names, the *Tetragram*[2] which is the most glorious — to be written *Adonai* — *El, Eloha, Elohim, Shadai* and *Zebaoth*. Anyone who erases even a letter of one of these is flogged.[3]

---

[1] One who cannot calculate and pay the tithes; the food is prohibited until this has been done.

[2] This Name is never uttered except by the High Priest on the Day of Atonement.

[3] Flogging, an appointed number of lashes, 39 for transgression of a negative commandment.

3.   Any prefix to these Names, such as the particles 'to' or 'from' may be erased for they do not sanctify the Name; but suffixes, such as 'thine' or 'yours' may not be erased for they are as sacred as the other letters of the Name, which sanctifies them. However, anyone who erases such a suffix, although it is forbidden to rub them out, is not flogged but gets the 'beating of a rebel'.[1]

4.   If the first two letters of the Name of God or the first two of the *Tetragram* are written, they may not be erased, and, needless to say, the last two letters of the *Tetragram* because they constitute the Name by themselves. The first two letters of *Shadai* and of *Zebaoth* may be erased.

5.   All other titles used to praise the Holy One, such as Gracious, Merciful, Great, Powerful, Terrible, Faithful, Zealous and Strong, and so on, are like other words of Holy Writ which may be erased.

6.   Utensils upon which the name is written must have the part cut out and buried with hidden texts[2] — even if the Name is engraved on vessels of metal or glass. If anyone re-casts such a vessel deliberately, he is flogged, for the engraved area must be cut out and buried. So also, if the Name is written on his body, he may not wash or anoint it or remain in a place which is dirty. If he is obliged to take a ritual bath, he must cover it with a leaf, and if no leaf is near, with his garment, and not fix it so that it gets in the way of the immersion. It was to be covered because it is forbidden to be naked in the presence of the Name.[3]

7.   Anyone who deliberately destroys even a stone of the Altar or Temple or its Court was flogged. For it says in connection with idolatry: 'Ye shall overthrow their altars' (of idolaters). 'Ye shall not do so unto the Lord your God' (Deuteronomy 12:3-4). Also anyone who burnt wood used for sacred purposes was lashed. For it was said that idolators' groves should be burned but 'Ye shall not do so unto the Lord your God'.

8.   It was forbidden to burn or deliberately destroy the Holy Scriptures, their commentaries and explanations. Whoever did so was whipped as a rebel. These rules applied to sacred writings written by a dedicated Israelite. If any unbeliever copied a book of the Torah it was burned along with

---

[1] Just a 'good beating'.

[2] In a *genizah;* see glossary.

[3] One way of discouraging tatooing which was strictly forbidden, as also was any custom of cutting the skin.

the names which were in it because he did not believe in the
Holy Name, did not write it for His Name's sake but merely
considered it an ordinary matter and therefore did not
'sanctify the Name'. It was a positive command to burn it in
order that the memory of the unbeliever and his work should
not remain. If a Gentile wrote the Holy Name it was buried
in a *genizah*.   Similarly, Holy Writ which a moth had
consumed or which a Gentile had written, were hidden.

9.   All the Names used by Abraham are sacred, even such as
'My Lord, if now I have found favour in thy sight' (Genesis
18:3). The Names used by Lot are profane except when he
said: 'Oh, not so, my Lord' (Genesis 19:18). All Names
associated with Geboth Benjamin are sacred (Judges 20): all
those connected with Micha are profane (Judges 17): all
Names associated with Naboth are sacred (I Kings 21). Every
Name in the Song of Songs of Solomon is sacred like the
other attributes except: 'Thou, O Solomon, must have a
thousand' (Song of Solomon 8:12). Every mention of a king
in Daniel is profane except: 'Thou, O king, art a king of
kings' (Daniel 2:37) which is like the other attributes.

Chapter 7

1.   It is a maxim of belief that God bestows prophecy[1] upon
the sons of men. But prophecy does not descend except upon
one of great wisdom and strong in character, not allowing
desires to control him but controlling them always, a man of
wide knowledge and very great integrity. One endowed with
these qualities and perfect health will, when he enters *Pardes*
and encounters great and profound subjects, possess correct
knowledge to understand and perceive; he will increase in
piety and will separate himself from the way of people who
walk in the darkness of their times. He is zealous and teaches
himself not to have empty thoughts of the vanities and
trivialities of the time. He keeps his mind free but lofty and
tied to the Lord's throne in order to understand holy and
pure ideas and to contemplate the wisdom of the Holy One —
blessed be He! — from the highest forms to the lowliest on

[1] Prophesy in ancient Israel did not predict the future as it means
in English today. De Quincy put it thus: 'It implied exegetic gifts, an
interpretation of what was dark, analysis applied to what is logistically
perplexed, expansion of what was condensed, practical improvement to
what might be overlooked as purely speculative'. *Confessions of an
English Opium Eater*, p 61 World's Classics Series.

earth, and to understand from them of His might. Then the Spirit of Holiness will rest on him and when the Spirit rests on him his soul will mingle with that of the messengers of the degree called *ishim*. He will then be transformed into another individual and understand that he is not as he was but is elevated above other wise men, as was said of Saul, 'thou shalt prophesy with them, and thou shalt be turned into another man' (I Samuel 10:6).

2.   Prophets are of different degrees. Just as one scholar is wiser that his fellow, so in prophecy, one prophet excels another in prophecy. They do not perceive the prophecy except in a dream or a vision by night, or in a trance by day as was said: 'I the Lord will make myself known unto him in a vision and will speak unto him in a dream' (Numbers 12:6). When they prophesy their limbs shake, their bodily strength fails, their thoughts are confused, but enough understanding remains to understand what is seen, as was said of Abraham, 'an horror of great darkness fell upon him' (Genesis 15:12), and of Daniel, 'I was left alone, and saw this great vision, and there remained no strength in me' (Daniel 10:8).

3.   The matters which are made known to a prophet in a vision are revealed as allegories. At once their meaning is engraved on the heart and he understands it, as Jacob our Father who saw the ladder with the messengers going up and down and knew that it was a parable of kingdoms rising and being enslaved (Genesis 28:12). Likewise Ezekial (1:5) saw 'creatures' and (2:9) 'a roll of a book', Jeremiah (1, 11, 13) 'a rod of an almond tree' and 'a seething pot', and Zachariah (2:1) 'a measuring line'. Similarly the other prophets saw things in visions. Some of them tell the parable and explain it, some only tell the explanation, some a parable without explanations as do Ezekeil and Zachariah. All of them prophesy in parables and with hidden meanings.

4.   Prophets do not all prophesy when they want to but must direct their minds and stay happy, and contented and alone. Prophecy does not dwell when there is distress or indolence but when there is gladness; therefore the disciples of the prophets had with them the psaltery, tabret, pipe and harp when they were seeking prophecy (I Samuel 10:5), as it was said they sought prophesy which meant they went in the path of prophecy until they prophesied. Today one would say so and so was growing up.

5.   Those who desire to prophesy are called sons of the prophets and, although they train their minds, it is uncertain

whether or not the *Shechinah* (see glossary) will rest upon them.

6. All these things which we speak of about prophecy refer to all the early and later prophets except Moses our teacher who was the greatest of them all. The difference between the prophecy of Moses and the others was that the others prophesied by means of dreams and visions but Moses our master prophesied when he was awake and standing up, as was said: 'And when Moses was gone into the tabernacle of the congregation to speak with Him, then he heard the voice of one speaking unto him' (Numbers 7:89). All the others received it from a messenger in the form of a parable or allegory. Moses our teacher did not receive it by a messenger, as was said: 'With him will I speak mouth to mouth' (Numbers 12:8), and it was also said: 'The Lord spake unto Moses face to face' (Exodus 33:11). Again it was said: 'the similitude of the Lord shall he behold' (Numbers 12:8), which means that there was no parable; he saw the matter perfectly without allegory or metaphor. The Torah bears witness that it was clear without any mystery; he did not prophesy in a secret way but saw with clear vision. All the other prophets were terrified, and trembled and became weak but Moses our master was not so. The verse says: 'As a man speaketh to his friend', meaning that no one trembles at the voice of his friend. Such was the strength of the mind of Moses our master to understand prophetic words that he stood up and was calm. All the other prophets could not prophesy at will. Moses our master was not thus but when he sought the Holy Spirit it covered him and prophecy fell upon him. He did not need to prepare himself and invite it, for he was always ready and prepared, as the ministering messengers are. He prophesied at all times, as was said: 'Stand still, and I will hear what the Lord will command concerning you' (Numbers 9:8). And the Almighty supported him saying: 'Go say to them, Get into your tents again. But as for thee, stand thou here by me' (Deuteronomy 5:30,31). Learn from this that when prophesy departed from prophets they returned to their tents for bodily needs like other people and were not separated from their wives. Moses our master did not so, he did not return to his former tent but separated for ever from his wife and such things and fixed his mind on the Rock of the Universe. Glory never left him and his face shone with rays of light and he was consecrated as the messengers are.

7.   It was possible that a prophet might prophesy for himself alone to broaden his understanding and increase his knowledge of great matters until he knew things that he did not know before. It was also possible that he might be sent to illiterate people or to the inhabitants of a city or to a government to direct it what to do or to prevent the evil which was in hand. When one was sent a sign or wonder was given to him in order that the people might know that in truth he had been sent by God. Not all those who performed a sign or miracle were believed to be prophets, only a man who was known well to us as worthy of prophecy on account of his wisdom and conduct — which excelled that of his colleagues — and who followed the path of prophecy in piety and abstinence. If after that he performed a sign or miracle and said that the Lord had sent him, it was a positive commandment to listen to him. It was said of such: 'Unto him ye shall hearken' (Deuteronomy 18:15). Yet it was possible that one might perform a sign or miracle and not be a prophet. The sign might have something unconvincing about it; yet it was a command to listen because he was great and wise and might be capable of prophecy, and of being supported because of his status. We may be commanded to follow him just as we have been commanded to accept a judgment based on the evidence of two worthy witnesses, even although possibly their witness might be false.   Because we considered them worthy we supported their integrity. In such and similar matters the verse states: 'The secret things belong unto the Lord our God; but those things which are revealed belong unto us and to our children' (Deuteronomy 29:29) and again: 'for man looketh on the outward appearance, but the Lord looketh on the heart' (I Samuel 16:7).

Chapter 8

1.   Moses our master was not trusted by Israel solely because of signs which he did, for whoever believes on account of signs retains a doubt in his heart that perhaps they were performed by magic and witchcraft. All the signs which Moses performed in the desert were done for necessities, not as manifestation of prophecy. It was necessary to drown the Egyptians; Moses divided the sea and he sank them in it. We needed food and he brought the manna down for us; when the people were thirsty he split the rock. When the Korah conspiracy denied him, the earth swallowed them, and it was

the same with the other signs. Why was he trusted? Because on Mount Sinai they saw with their own eyes and heard through their own ears — not through a stranger's ears — the fire and the thunder and lightning as he approached the cloud and they heard the voice saying 'Moses, Moses go and tell them such and such things'. So he spoke face to face with the Lord (Deuteronomy 5:4) and it was said: 'The Lord made not this convenant with our fathers, but with us' (Deuteronomy 5:3). How do we know that the standing alone on Mount Sinai was a true manifestation of his prophecy in which there was no shadow of doubt? Because it was said: 'Lo, I come unto thee in a thick cloud, that the people may hear when I speak with thee, and believe in thee for ever' (Exodus 19:9). Before this they evidently did not trust him with genuine truth merely with belief, which has after-thoughts and doubt.

2. So it was that they, to whom Moses was sent, were witnesses of his prophecy, that it was true, and there was no need for him to make any other sign. For they and he witnessed it together, just as two witnesses see something together and each gives evidence that the other speaks the truth, and there is no need for one to prove what the other saw. Thus all Israel witnessed with him on Mount Sinai and there was no need for him to give a sign. This was what the Holy One — blessed be He! — said at the beginning of Moses's prophecy when He gave him the signs which he performed in Egypt saying: 'And they shall hearken to thy voice' (Exodus 3:18). Moses our teacher knew that whoever depends upon miracles has in his heart doubts, thoughts and reflections, just as he when he himself tried to avoid going to the people and said: 'But, behold, they will not believe me' (Exodus 4:1).

Then the Holy One — blessed be He! — made known to him that these signs were only needed to get them out of Egypt and that after that, when they stood upon the mountain the suspicious thoughts which they had about him would cease. In that way He gave Moses the sign that He had in truth sent him from the beginning and no doubts would remain in their hearts. This is what is written: '. . . This shall be a token unto thee that I have sent thee when thou hast brought forth the people out of Egypt, ye shall serve God upon this mountain' (Exodus 3:12). Thus any prophet arising after Moses our teacher should not be trusted on account of signs only — as if saying when he performs a miracle we will

listen to everything he says — but because of the commandment of Moses in the Torah that if he gives a sign we must
listen. In the same way as we have to establish a matter on
the evidence of two witnesses, — although we do not know
whether their witness is true or false, — we have to listen to
such a prophet, and this even although we do not know
whether the sign is true or performed by magic and witchcraft (Deuteronomy 18:15).

3. If therefore a prophet arises and performs signs and
great wonders, and seek to deny the prophecy of Moses our
teacher, we do not listen for we know clearly that his tokens
are enchantment and witchcraft. Moses's prophecy does not
depend upon wonders which are compared with the wonders
performed by others, for with our eyes we saw, and with our
ears we heard, what we heard. Know that this is comparable
to the evidence of witnesses who testify for another that
what he himself saw with his own eyes was not so, and we do
not listen because certainly it is false evidence. Therefore it
is said in the Torah that even if signs and wonders come to
pass 'thou shalt not hearken unto the words of that prophet'
(Deuteronomy 13:3), for he comes with signs and wonders to
deny what you saw with your own eyes. We do not believe
in miracles except in accordance with the commandments
which Moses gave us. How could we accept a sign brought to
deny the prophecy of Moses which we saw and heard?

Chapter 9

1. It is clearly stated in the Torah that it contains the Law
which stands for ever, that may not be changed, and nothing
may be taken from it or added ot it, as the Law said: 'What
thing soever I command you, observe to do it; thou shalt not
add thereto, nor diminish from it' (Deuteronomy 12:32), and
further, 'those things which are revealed belong unto us and
to our children forever, that we may do all the words of this
law' (Deuteronomy 29:29). We learn from this that all the
words of the Torah command us to do them for ever. It says
also: 'An ordinance for ever in your generations' (Numbers
15:15) and again: '(This commandment) it is not in heaven
... it is very nigh unto thee in thy mouth and in thy heart
that thou mayest do it', (Deuteronomy 30:12-14). Learn
therefore that no prophet is allowed to make any change and,
if anyone stands up, whether a Gentile or Israelite, and gives
a sign and says that the Lord has sent him to add a command

or take one away or make an interpretation different from that of Moses, or who says that the commands which Israel was given are not everlasting but were in keeping with the times only, certainly he is a false prophet because he came to contradict the prophecy of Moses. He shall die by hanging because he deliberately spoke in the name of God what He had not commanded him. For the Holy One — blessed be He! — commanded Moses that these commandments 'belong unto us and to our children for ever' (Deuteronomy 29:29), and 'God is not a man that he should lie' (Numbers 23:19).

2. If that is so, why does the Torah say: 'I will raise them up a Prophet from among their brethren like unto thee' (Deuteronomy 18:18). This prophet is not to make new laws, rather to issue commands according to the Torah, and to warn the people not to transgress it. The last prophet said: 'Remember ye the law of Moses My servant' (Malachi 4:4). In the same way, in public duties if he is commanded 'go to such and such a place', 'join battle today' or 'build a fortress' or 'don't do these things', it is mandatory to listen and whoever does not do so deserves death from Heaven![1] For it is said: 'And it shall come to pass that whosoever will not hearken unto my words which he (the prophet) speak in my name, I will require it of him' (Deuteronomy 18:19).

3. Likewise a prophet who himself transgresses his own words or hides his prophecy deserves death from Heaven and of the three cases it says: 'I will require it of him'. Also if a prophet who is known to us to be a prophet tells us to transgress one or all of the commandments of the Torah whether small or great, one must listen for the moment. We have learned by tradition from the early sages that if a prophet tells you to transgress the words of the Torah as Elijah did on Mount Carmel, 'we must listen to him except in matters relating to idolatry'. Elijah had made a burnt offering on Mount Carmel when Jerusalem was the chosen place and anyone sacrificing outside it deserved excommunication.[2] However, because he was a prophet it was a duty to listen to him, even as was said: 'unto him ye shall hearken' (Deuteronomy 18:15). If they had asked Elijah how they could uproot what was in the Torah 'Take heed to thyself that thou offer not thy burnt offerings in every place'? (Deuteronomy 12:13), he would have answered that the world applied to one who was continually sacrificing in

---

[1] May mean that life is shortened.
[2] Either from God or the Community.

any place and deserved excommunication as Moses had commanded, but I am sacrificing outside today in the name of the Lord to confound the prophets of Baal. In this matter if any one of the prophets commands a temporary violation of a Law, one must listen. But if he says that the Law is to be uprooted for ever, he is hanged because the Torah 'is unto us and to our children for ever' (Deuteronomy 29:29).

4.   In the same way if he uproots any of our verbal traditions or says that God had charged him to interpret the Law in such and such a way, he is a false prophet and is to be hanged even although he gives a sign. For he came to deny the Torah, of which it was said: 'It is not in heaven ... but is very nigh unto thee' (Deuteronomy 30:12-14).   In a temporary matter he may be listened to.

5.   This holds for all commandments except those about idolatry when he, the prophet, may never be listened to even temporarily, and even if he performs signs and great miracles and claims that God has commanded him to worship idols only on a certain day or hour. This is rebellion against the Lord and concerning it there is written: 'And the sign or the wonder came to pass ... Thou shalt not hearken unto the words of that prophet' (Deuteronomy 13:2-3). For he has uttered rebellion against the Lord your God and has come to deny prophecy of Moses. Then we know for certain that he is false and that all he does is magic and witchcraft and that he should be hanged.

Chapter 10

1.   If a prophet arises among us and claims that God sent him, it is not necessary for him to deliver a sign like one of the tokens of Moses, our teacher, or Elijah or Elisha wherein were changes in natural law. But his predictions should be words about future happenings in the world and his words should come true. Will you say in your hearts: 'How shall we know the word which the Lord hath not spoken?' (Deuteronomy 18:21). If one comes who is worthy to prophesy, as a servant of the Name, and does not add or take away anything but advocates only the Lord's service in the commands of the Torah, we must not ask him to divide the sea or raise the dead so that we may believe him. But we may say to him, 'if you are a prophet tell us about future things' and, if he does, we wait and see whether they are fulfilled

or not; even if a small part of his prophecy fails, he is false. But if all his prophecy comes to pass, our eyes are witness to his truth.

2. We examine him many times and, if all his words are true, he is a true prophet, as was said of Samuel: 'All Israel from Dan even to Beer-sheba knew that Samuel was established to be a prophet of the Lord' (I Samuel 3:20).

3. But are not the magicians and enchanters predicting the future? So what is the difference between them and the prophets? The magicians and enchanters and their like utter predictions which are partly true and partly not. And perhaps some of their words will be fulfilled and some may not. As the verse says: 'Let now the astrologers, the stargazers, the monthly prognosticators, stand up, and save thee from these things that shall come upon thee' (Isaiah 47:13). It is possible that their words may not be established but are completely wrong, as was said: 'I am the Lord that ... frustrateth the tokens of the liars and maketh diviners mad; and ... maketh their knowledge foolish' (Isaiah 44:24-26). But all the words of a prophet are established, as was said: 'Know now that there shall fall unto the earth nothing of the word of the Lord' (2 Kings 10:10), and again: 'The prophet that hath a dream, let him tell a dream; and he that hath my word, let him speak my word faithfully. What is the chaff to the wheat? saith the Lord' (Jeremiah 23:28). This means that the words of the magicians and dreamers are like chaff which have a little grain mixed with them but the word of the Lord is like grain in which there is no chaff at all. The verse truly confirms that the sayings of the soothsayers and astrologers to the nations are lies, but the prophet makes truth known to them and there is no need for soothsayers and magicians and the like. The verse says, 'There shall not be found among you any that maketh his son or his daughter to pass through the fire ...' (Deuteronomy 18:10). Learn you this, that a prophet will only arise among us to make known what the future will bring to the world such as plenty, or famine, war, or peace and like matters. Individual needs may be known to him. For example, when Saul lost some things he went to a prophet to be told where it was (I Samuel 9:1-9). A prophet may tell such things, but he may not invent new belief or add to or diminish a commandment.

4. When a prophet predicts calamities, for example that so and so will die or that in such a year there will be famine or war and these do not happen, it does not deny him as a

prophet. No one may say: 'Behold his word is not fulfilled'. The Holy One — blessed be He! — is slow to anger and very generous and repents of evil and possibly there may be repentance and forgiveness, as happened to the men of Nineveh (Jonah 3:5-8); or delay as in the case of Hezekiah (Isaiah 38:4). But if the prophet is sure that good will come and such and such will happen and the good does not come, he surely is a false prophet; for all good is an edict of God and, even if there is a stipulation, He does not go back on that. We do not find that He went back on any good except when the first Temple was destroyed when He promised the righteous that they would not die with the wicked. He retracted evidently, as is explained in the Treatise on the Sabbath.[1] Learn from this, that a prophet can be tested on good news only, as Jeremiah said in his answer to Hananiah son of Azur when he, Jeremiah, was prophesying evil and Hananiah good. 'The prophets that have been before me and before thee of old prophesied both against many countries and many kingdoms, of war, and of evil, and of pestilence. The prophet which prophesied of peace, when the word of the prophet shall come to pass, then shall the prophet be known that the Lord hath truly sent him' (Jeremiah 28:8,9).
5. A prophet who is attested by another prophet as genuine needs no second investigation. For did not Moses our teacher vouch for the faithfulness of Joshua, and all Israel believed in him before he made any sign, and so through the generations. A prophet whose prophecy is known and his words believed over and over again, or of whom another prophet has testified that he has continued in the path of prophecy, may not be doubted or his prophecy held in suspicion that it is false. It is forbidden to test him more than necessary or to go on testing him for ever, as it was written: 'Ye shall not tempt the Lord your God as ye tempted Him in Massah' (Deuteronomy 6:16), as when the children of Israel said: 'Is the Lord among us, or not?' (Exodus 17:7). But when a prophet is recognised it must be believed that the Lord is among them and there must not be suspicion about him, as the verse said: 'They shall know that there hath been a prophet among them' (Ezekiel 2:5).

Here ends Treatise 1 on the Foundation of the Torah.

---

[1] Wickedness was great and the righteous did not rebuke the evil-doers sufficiently.

Treatise 2
DISCERNMENT[1]

In this eleven commandments (five positive and six negative) are explained, and they are:

1. To imitate the ways of the Lord.
2. To keep close to those who have knowledge of Him.
3. To love neighbours.
4. To love strangers.
5. Not to hate neighbours.
6. To rebuke a wrongdoer.
7. Not to put anyone to shame.
8. Not to humiliate the unfortunate.
9. Not to be a tale bearer.
10. Not to take revenge.
11. Not to bear a grudge.

Chapter 1

1.   There are many widely different temperaments among the children of men. There is the hot tempered man who is always angry and the calm man, serene in disposition who is never angry, or if he shows anger, it is only a little anger in many years. One man is arrogant, another quite humble; one is obsessed by desire and never satisfied, another so pure in heart that he does not even long for the few needs of the body. There is the greedy man who would never be satisfied with all the wealth in the world, as the saying goes 'He that loveth silver shall not be satisfied with silver' (Ecclesiastes 5:10). Another shortens his life because he is satisfied with the little which is insufficient for his needs and will not look for or try to get what he needs. One will mortify himself to starvation, hoard everything and will not eat a pennyworth without pain to himself, while another scatters his goods as he fancies. So it is with all the temperaments, for example, cheerfulness and gloom, miserliness and generosity, cruelty and kindness, timidity and courage, and so on.

[1] See glossary

28

2.   Between all these extremes there are intermediate degrees which differ from each other. There are some dispositions which are inborn in man and depend upon the nature of his body and these predispose him to certain temperaments. Others are not inherited but are learned from other men or selected because of some ideas in the heart, or because a man has heard that this trend would be good for him, and he thinks it proper, and he conducts himself accordingly until it is fixed in his heart.

3.   The two opposite extremes in all dispositions are not the good way, and it is not fitting for a man to follow them or to be instructed in them. If a man finds his nature tending towards one of them, or ready for one of them, or has already learned it, and conducts himself accordingly he turns himself towards goodness and goes along the path of the good which is the straight path.

4.   The right way is the middle path. It is found in all dispositions of man and is equally removed from both extremes and is not near to either. For this reason the ancient sages commanded that man should examine his inclinations continually, weigh them and direct them intentionally to the middle path in order to have a sound body. For example, one ought not to be a hot tempered man and given to anger, nor without feeling like the dead, but between the two, not becoming enraged except in a great matter when anger is needed to prevent something happening again. So also he should only crave for what the body requires and cannot live without, as was said: 'The righteous eateth to the satisfying of his soul' (Proverbs 13:25). Likewise he ought not to toil at his business but acquire what is necessary for life from day to day, as the saying goes: 'A little that a righteous man hath is better than the riches of many wicked' (Psalm 37:16). He ought not to be too tight-fisted nor squander his money but give charity within his means and lend to one in need. He should not be always cheerful and laughing nor distressed and mournful, but should be glad all his days in moderation, and receive all men with a friendly countenance. So should it be with all the different dispositions for that is the path of wise men. Men of equanimity are called wise.

5.   The man who is excessively critical of himself and leaves the middle path, tending towards one extreme or another, is called pious. For example, one who abandons arrogance and goes to the other extreme of humility is called pious, for that is the character of piety. If one keeps in the middle path and

is also humble, one is called wise, for that is the characteristic of wisdom. This applies in all dispositions. The ancient pious men turned from the mean towards the two extremes, some leaning towards piety others towards wisdom more than is demanded by the Law. We however are required to go in the middle paths for they are good and straight, as was said: 'walk in His ways' (Deuteronomy 28:9).

6.   Concerning this command the teaching was thus; even as God is called gracious, be thou gracious; even as He is called merciful, be thou merciful; even as He is called holy, be thou holy. In this way the prophets gave attributes to God such as 'slow to anger', 'of great mercy', 'righteous', 'upright', 'perfect', 'mighty' and 'strong' and so on, in order to make known that these are the good and straight paths which it is the duty of a man to follow and so to be like the Lord, as far as he is able.

7.   How does a man accustom himself to these dispositions until they are fixed in him? He should do once, twice and thrice the things that belong to the middle path and repeat them until they become easy for him and need no effort. Then they become rooted in his soul. Because these attributes are applied to the Creator and are the middle way which we must follow, they are called the Lord's way. This was how Abraham had instructed his children when the Lord said: 'I know him that he will command his children and his household after him, and they shall keep the way of the Lord' (Genesis 18:19). He who follows this way brings well being and blessing to himself, so 'that the Lord may bring upon Abraham that which he hath spoken of him' (Genesis 18:19).

Chapter 2

1.   To a sick man the bitter may taste sweet and sweet bitter, and a person who is ill may crave for things which are not suitable to eat such as dust and charcoal, and may hate good things like a piece of bread and meat, according to the type of his sickness. In the same way those who are sick in soul crave for and love evil tendencies and hate the path of good. They are lazy and the path is too arduous for them in proportion to their sickness. Isaiah says of them: 'Woe unto them that call evil good, and good evil; that put darkness for light, and light for darkness: that put bitter for sweet, and sweet for bitter' (Isaiah 5:20). Concerning those it says: 'Who

leave the path of uprightness to walk in the ways of darkness' (Proverbs 2:13). How is the sick soul to be repaired? He must go to the wise, the physicians of the soul, who heal by disciplines that they teach, until he is brought back to the good way. Of those who recognise their evil incliniations and do not consult the wise for healing, Solomon said: 'fools despise wisdom and instruction' (Proverbs 1:7).

2. How can they be cured? We tell the hot tempered man that he must accustom himself to be smitten and abused without feeling anything, and continue in that way for a long time until the ill temper is rooted out of his heart. If a man is conceited, he must discipline himself to be shamed and to sit beneath others and to dress himself in ragged clothes that degrade the wearers and likewise in other matters until he uproots the pride from his heart and returns to the good middle path. When he returns to the middle way he should follow it all his days, and this line should be followed by men of all the different temperaments. If a man has gone to one extreme, let him go to the other and conduct himself that way for a long time, until he returns to the good path which is the middle way in each temperament.

3. Yet there are some temperaments where man is forbidden to follow in the middle way but must go from one extreme to the opposite. An example is pride. For the good way here is not only that a man must be humble[1] but also of a very lowly spirit. In this connection it was said of Moses our teacher that he was not only meek, but was very meek (Numbers 12:3). Therefore the sages commanded saying 'be very, very lowly of spirit' and they further stated that all pride denies the existence of God, as was said: 'Then thine heart be lifted up, and thou forget the Lord thy God' (Deuteronomy 8:14). The rabbis also said: 'Excommunicate him who has even a little of the haughty spirit'. Anger also is a very evil tendency and it is essential for a man to remove himself to the other extreme, to teach himself not to be angry even about something which he ought to be angry about. If one wants to instil awe into one's children and household, or into the public if one is a leader, and wishes to be angry with them so that they may return to good ways, one should appear before them as angry only to reprove them, but one's disposition must be calm as a man imitating anger when he should be angry, but in reality he is not angry. The sages of old said that 'he who is angry is as if he

[1] Opposite of aggressive and arrogant.

worshipped idols'. They said that 'if a wise man became enraged his wisdom left him and prophecy deserted a prophet if he became enraged'. The life of an angry man is no life. The advice was to keep away from anger and train oneself not to feel even things which are enraging for that is the good path. The way of the upright is to be insulted but not to give insult, to hear abuse but not to answer, to do their duty as a work of love and be cheerful in suffering. Of them the verse states: 'Let them that love Him be as the sun when he goeth forth in his might' (Judges 5:31).

4.   At all times a man should cultivate silence and ought not to speak except when he has something wise to say or something necessary for life. They said of Rab the pupil of our Holy Master[1] that all his days he never in his life uttered idle talk — which is the conversation of most people. A man should not multiply words about bodily needs, and the sages said that 'he who multiplies words leads to sin'; and also, 'I found nothing better for bodily well being than silence'. Also the words of the Torah and wisdom said that the speech of man ought to be little and its contents great; that is what the sages commanded when they said 'a master should teach his pupils briefly'. If words are many and their contents little, they are foolish; of such it was said 'For a dream cometh from a multitude of business; and a fool's voice is known by multitude of words.' (Ecclesiastes 5:3).

5.   Silence is the rampart of wisdom and one ought not to hurry to answer or multiply words. One should teach pupils restfully and quietly without shouting and long words. As Solomon said 'The words of wise men are heard in quiet' (Ecclesiastes 9:17).

6.   A man is forbidden to accustom himself to flattery and seduction, and he may not say one thing with his mouth and have another in his heart, but what is within must be as what is without. What is in his heart shall be in his mouth, and it is forbidden to steal or deceive the mind of any one even that of a non Jew. For example one may not sell to a non Jew the flesh or a shoe thong of an animal which died of itself in place of one ritually slaughtered and conceal that the death was not brought about by slaughter. One may not urge one's friend to eat with one when one knows that he will not, or tempt him with dainties which he will not accept, and one should not open a cask of wine for trade and pretend that it was in another's honour, and so on. Even one word of

[1] Judah the Patriarch, author of the Mishanah of the 2nd century.

32

seduction and deceit is forbidden. Be true in speech, upright in spirit and keep a pure heart and be clear of mischief and ill will.

7. A man must not be frivolous and sarcastic, or sad and miserable, but cheerful. The wise fathers said that laughter and frivolity lead a man to lewdness and they commanded that one ought not to be boisterous in laughter nor desolate and miserable but should greet every one with a friendly face. Also a man ought not to be greedy and always hurrying after wealth, and not lazy and neglectful of work, but he ought to keep a kindly eye, not over busy, but occupied with the Torah and he should rejoice in his small portion. He must not be argumentative, envious, covetous or run after honour. The wise fathers said that envy, desire and fame remove man from the world and shorten life. The general principle in this matter is to follow the middle paths of each disposition until they become fixed. Solomon said on this subject: 'Ponder the path of they feet, and let all thy ways be established' (Proverbs 4:26).

Chapter 3

1. Should a man say: 'since envy and lust and glory and such like are evil and shorten his life, I shall remove myself to the other extreme and not eat meat, not drink wine, not marry, not live in a pleasant place, and not dress nicely, but in a sack of coarse wool, as some of the heathen priests do'. That is an evil way in which it is forbidden to go and he who follows it is called a sinner for the verse states of the Nazarite: 'The priest shall make an atonement for him, for that he sinned by the deed', (Numbers 6:11), and the sages said that, if the Nazarite requires atonement for separating himself only from wine, how much more so the person who denies himself all other things. Because of this the sages said that man should not deny himself anything except what was commanded in the Torah, and not forbid himself by vows and oaths from things allowed to him. They said: 'Is it not enough for you what the Torah has forbidden that you should deny yourself other things?'. In general this included those who afflict themselves by fasting; they are not in the good way. The sages forbade a man to punish himself by fasting. Of such things, Solomon advised: 'Be not righteous over much; neither make thyself over wise; why shouldest thou destroy thyself?' (Ecclesiastes 7:16).

2. It is necessary for man to direct his heart and deeds to know and understand the Holy Name — blessed be He! — so that in sitting, standing and in speaking he should be aligned thus. For example in business and in doing work for wages, he should not only think of getting money but do these things in order to have what is necessary for the body, such as food and drink and a dwelling and marriage. In the same way, when he eats and drinks and enjoys marital intercourse he should not set his heart on doing them for pleasure only, until he finds that he eats and drinks just for the delight of the palate, and has intercourse just for pleasure, but should aim at eating and drinking to keep his body and limbs healthy. Therefore he ought not to eat every time that his palate craves, like a dog or a donkey. He should eat what is most useful for the body, whether bitter or sweet, and not eat anything bad for the body, although it may be sweet to the taste. For example, whoever has fever ought not to eat meat and honey or drink wine, as Solomon said in a proverb: 'It is not good to eat too much honey[1] (Proverbs 25:27). He should have a drink of chicory, although it is bitter. He should be found eating and drinking in a healthy way only in order that he may recover and remain sound, because it is impossible for a man to live without food and drink. Likewise in intercourse he should have it only for bodily health and to propagate the race. On this account he should not have intercourse every time he desires but when it is needed for good health or to get descendants.

3. Whoever conducts himself solely for health and sets his heart on having body and limbs sound and on having children to do his work and toil for his needs, is not in the good path. He must set his desire on a healthy, strong body, in order that his spirit may be upright and have knowledge of God, for it is not possible to understand and be equipped for wisdom if one is hungry, or sick, or if one has pain in a limb. A man should aspire to have a son who may be perhaps a wise and great man in Israel. He who follows this path all his days serves the Lord always, even when he is buying and selling or having marital intercourse because his thoughts' desire is that he should have enough to keep his body healthy to serve God. Even in sleep, if he sleeps in order to rest his mind and body so that he may not become sick and unable to serve God, this is found to serve God — blessed be He! On this subject the sages commanded and said: 'Let all thy deeds

---

[1] Perhaps implying 'to much of a good thing'.

34

be for the sake of Heaven', and Solomon in his wisdom said: 'In all thy ways acknowledge him and he shall direct thy paths' (Proverbs 3:6).

Chapter 4

1. It follows that a healthy and sound body is in the Lord's path, for it is impossible to understand or grasp knowledge of the Creator if one is sick. For that reason it is important to remove oneself from things that injure the body and to accustom oneself to things which are healthy and sustaining. These are only to eat when hungry, and not to drink unless thirsty, not to delay bodily eliminations, even for a short time, but always to rise at once when it is necessary to urinate or evacuate.

2. Man ought not to eat until his stomach is full but stop short of satiety by one quarter. He must not drink water with his food except a little mixed with wine. When the food begins to be digested, he may drink what he needs but not too much water even after digestion has started. He should not eat until he is sure that it is not necessary to go to the privy. A man ought not to eat until he has warmed up his body by working or otherwise tiring himself. In general he should work and tire his body every day in the morning until it is warm and he perspires a little. Then he should compose himself and eat. If he has a hot bath after fatigue that is good and he ought to rest a little before eating.

3. After eating a man should sit where he is or lean on his left side and neither walk nor ride, not tire himself or shake himself up or stroll about until digestion is finished. Those who wander about after eating and tire themselves invite grave and serious diseases.

4. Day and night consist of twenty-four hours and it is enough for a man to sleep a third of that, namely eight hours, and sleep should be at the end of the night so that he rises from his bed before the sun appears.

5. A man ought not to sleep on his face or on his back but on his side; at the beginning of the night on the left side and at the end on the right side. He ought not to sleep at once after food but wait for three or four hours thereafter, and he ought not to sleep during the day.

6. Things which loosen the bowels like grapes, figs, berries, pears, and varieties of melon and cucumber, should be eaten before the main meal, not mixed with it. One should then

wait a little until these pass down and then partake the meal. Substances which stiffen the bowels, such as pomegranate, quince, apricots and curdled foods, may be eaten at once after a meal but not to excess.

7. When one wishes to eat the flesh of both bird and domestic animal at the same meal, he should eat of the bird first. Similarly with eggs and poultry, the egg should be taken first. Thus, with the flesh of small and large animals, the former should be eaten first; always the lighter foods before the heavier.

8. In the hot season cool food should be eaten without spices but with some vinegar. In the rainy season warm food with spices and a little mustard, and asafoetida. In cold and warm climates one should do what is suitable in each.

9. There are some foods which are extremely bad and they ought never to be eaten. For example, large, long-salted fishes, and old salt cheese, truffles and mushrooms, and long-salted meat and unfermented wine, or any cooked food kept until it emits a smell. Indeed all food which has an unpleasant smell or is very bitter is like deadly poison to the body. There are also some foods which are not good but not as bad as the above. It is desirable for man to eat only a little of them and only occasionally, and he ought not to become accustomed to them and make his regular meals of them: for example large fishes, cheese, and milk milked more than twenty four hours previously, the flesh of big oxen and rams. Beans, peas, lentils, barley bread, unleavened bread, cabbage, leeks, onions, garlic, mustard and radish are all bad and it is not good to take them except in small quantities and in the rainy season. But in hot weather one ought not to eat them at all. Peas and beans are not suitable for either hot or rainy seasons. Gourds are food for hot days.

10. There are other bad foods which are not as bad as those previously mentioned. They are water fowl, young pigeons, dates, and break soaked and kneaded with oil, and grain finely ground so that no scent of the husk remains, sauces and also pickles. It is not good to eat these often. A wise man who controls his desires and does not give way to his inclinations and does not partake of these mentioned foods at all except for medicinal purposes — he is indeed strong!

11. A man should refrain from eating the fruits of trees and not eat much of them even when dried or, needless to say, when juicy. Unripe fruits are like swords to the body. Locust beans are always bad. Acid fruits are also bad and must be

consumed in small quantities in the hot weather or hot climates. Figs and grapes and almonds are always good to eat whether ripe or dried, and one may eat what one requires of them but may not eat them continually although they are better than all other fruits of trees.

12.   Honey and wine are bad for children and good for the aged, especially in the rainy season. In the summer a man should only eat two thirds of what he eats in the rainy season.

13.   One should be careful to keep the bowels loose always, almost near to diarrhoea. In general it is recognised in medicine that if elimination is prevented or difficult, serious illness is approaching. How can one cure constipation? If he is young, he must eat every morning something salted and soaked in olive oil or rubbed in salt, but no bread. He may drink water in which spinach has been cooked or locust beans in olive oil and salted. If he is old, he should drink honey mixed in warm water in the morning and wait for four hours before the morning meal and continue this for one or three or four days until the bowels loosen.

14.   Still another general rule is advised about bodily health. So long as a man works and tires himself out, does not eat to satiety and his bowels are loose, illness will not come to him and his strength shall be renewed, even if he eats bad foods.

15.   Whoever sits idle and does not tire himself and delays his eliminations and is constipated, even if he eats good foods and keeps medical rules, shall have pains all his days and his strength shall weaken. Gross feeding is to the body of man as a deadly poison and it is the root of all illness. Many of the diseases which overtake man are due either to eating bad food or because he fills himself grossly full, even of good food. Solomon said in his wisdom: 'Whoso keepeth his mouth and his tongue keepeth his soul from troubles' (Proverbs 21:23). That is to say, guard your mouth from bad food and overeating and your tongue from speaking, except when needful.

16.   Proper bathing. This should be once every seven days but not at meal times or when one is hungry, but after food has begun to digest. The whole body should be washed with hot water that does not scald the body, except the head which may be washed with water that would scald the body. After that a man should wash in luke warm, then cooler and finally cold water, but he should not pass over his head either luke-warm or cold water. In the rainy season cold water

should not be used. He should not bathe till he sweats and wears out all his body, nor remain in the bath house long, but as soon as he begins to perspire and feel relaxed he should have a shower and go out. He must examine himself before and after the bath, whether evacuation is needed, in the same way before and after meals, before and after marital intercourse, before and after fatiguing toil, before and after sleep: that is ten times.

17. When a man leaves the bath house, he should dress himself and cover his head in the outer room that he may not be overcome by a cold wind; even in hot weather it is necessary to be careful. He should delay a little until he is composed in spirit and rested in body and loses heat, and then he may eat. If he sleeps a little after the bath before eating, so much the better. He ought not to drink cold water immediately after leaving the bath house and needless to say he ought not to drink in the bath. If he is thirsty on coming out of the bath and cannot resist it, he should mix water and wine or honey and drink that. If he covers himself with oil in the bath house in cold weather after the shower, that also is good.

18. A man ought not to accustom himself to bloodletting. He ought not to let blood except when very necessary. He ought not to bloodlet in hot weather or during the rains but a little in the spring during the days of *nisan* and a little in autumn during the days of *tishri*. After fifty years of age he ought not to let blood and not on the day when he bathes, or goes on a journey or returns from a journey. On the day of bloodletting he ought to eat and drink less than usual, should rest and not exhaust himself or take a walk.

19. Emission of seed is the strength of the body, its life, and it is part of the brightness of the eyes; but in excess it diminishes the body and strength and life is destroyed. As Solomon, in his wisdom, said: 'Give not thy strength unto women' (Proverbs 31:3). Whoever cohabits to excess becomes prematurely old, his strength fails and his eyes become dim. An unpleasant odour comes from his mouth and armpits. The hairs of his head, eyebrows and eyelashes fall out, and the hair of the armpit and of the leg thicken. His teeth fall out and many other ailments beyond these come upon him. The wise physicians said: 'One in a thousand dies of other diseases, the rest of the thousand of sexual overindulgence'. So one should be warned about this if one wishes to lead a good life; one ought not to have

intercourse except when the body is healthy and very strong. If a man is preoccupied with this matter and, although he tries to think of other things, it is still there and he finds a weight from his loins downwards, as if cords of the testes were pulling and he is feverish, such a man needs intercourse and it will heal him. A man should not have intercourse when sated or hungry but when the food is digested and care should be taken to make empty the bowel before and after intercourse. It must not be when standing or sitting, not in a bath house and not on the day when one bathes, not on the day of bloodletting or going on a journey or arriving from a journey, neither before nor after these.

20. Whoever accustoms himself in these ways which I have explained, I guarantee that he will not have illness all his days until he dies in old age. He will need no physician and his body will be sound and remain healthy all his days, unless his body is unhealthy from its beginning or there was a diathesis which was bad from his birth, or if a plague or famine comes to the world.

21. All these good rules which we have advised are only applicable to the healthy. The sick man or one who has a painful limb or has had a bad habit for many years, for all such there are other paths and rules according to the disease; this is made clear in the book of medicines. Any change and disturbance in life's routine is the origin of sickness.

22. In any place where there is no doctor whether one is healthy or sick, it is undesirable to deviate from the rules enumerated in this chapter because every one of these brings good in the end.

23. In a city where ten things are not in existence, a wise man may not dwell. These are a physician, a surgeon, a bath house, a privy, running water such as a river or a spring, a synagogue, a teacher for the young, a clerk, a collector for charity and a law court and prison.

Chapter 5

1. In the same way as a wise man is recognised by his wisdom and discernment, which differentiates him from other people, so it is necessary for him to be recognised by his conduct, eating and drinking, marital relations, eliminations, speech, gait, dress, moderate language and in his business dealings. In all these matters he should be pleasant

and very particular. For example, a wise man must not be a glutton but eat what is sufficient for his bodily health and not grossly of that. He should not hurry to fill his stomach as those do who fill up with food and drink until their bellies swell. Of them tradition says: 'I will ... and spread dung upon your faces' (Malachi 2:3) and the sages said they are the people who eat and drink and make all days a festival and say: 'let us eat and drink; for tomorrow we shall die' (Isaiah 22:13). That is how the wicked eat and their tables are shamed by the verse which says that 'For all tables are full of vomit and filthiness, so that there is no place clean' (Isaiah 28:8). The wise man does not eat but one or two dishes and of them sufficient for life's need, as Solomon said: 'The righteous eateth to the satisfying of his soul' (Proverbs 13:25).

2.   When the wise man eats the little that he needs, he ought not to eat it anywhere except in his own house at his own table. He should not eat in an inn or in the market, except in extreme necessity, that he may not be undignified before the people. He should not eat with the illiterate and at tables full of filthy vomit nor eat his meals outside even with the wise, and he should not eat at large gatherings. It is improper for him to eat thus except at mandatory festivals such as betrothals and weddings and then only when a son of a scholar marries the daughter of a scholar. The righteous and pious of old never ate a meal which was not their own.

3.   When a wise man drinks wine he only takes sufficient to soften the food within him. Whoever becomes drunk, it is a sin and shameful and causes him to lose his wisdom. If he intoxicates himself before illiterate people, that is to profane the Holy Name. It is forbidden to drink wine at midday, even a little, except along with a meal, for drink with a meal is not intoxicating. No care is advised except for wine after a meal.

4.   Although a man's wife is always lawful to him, it is proper for a scholar to conduct himself in a holy way and not to have access to his wife like a cock but at each Sabbath night, if he has the vigour. When he has intercourse with her it should not be at the beginning of the night when he is well fed and his stomach full and not late when he is hungry, but in the middle of the night when digestion is over; not in frivolity and demeaning his mouth with indecent words, even between themselves. Indeed according to tradition 'the prudent shall keep silent' (Amos 4:13). This is interpreted by the sages thus: 'Even indecent conversation between a man

and his wife will have to be accounted for in the future'. Neither of them may be intoxicated, nor unwilling, nor grieving, and not when she is asleep. She may not be forced when unwilling but when both are consenting and happy, with a few pleasantries in order that she may be composed and not embarrassed, and not with violence and sudden break off.

5. Anyone who accustoms himself to this behaviour not only sanctifies and purifies himself but improves his understanding, so that if he has children they may be pleasant and modest, and worthy of wisdom and piety. But those who accustom themselves as do the people who go in darkness will have children like themselves.

6. The scholar trains himself to observe much decency, not to degrade himself nor to expose his head and body. Even on entering the privy he should act with decency, not expose himself when sitting or use his right hand to clean himself. He should remove himself from others and enter an inner room or cave and relieve himself or, if it be beyond the fence, he must distance himself so that his friend will not hear him if he sneezes. If he relieves himself in a valley, he must distance himself so that no one may see anything. He ought not to talk when relieving himself, even if there is great need. In the same modest way as he conducts himself by day in the privy, he should accustom himself to do by night and train himself to relieve himself thus in the morning and evening only, to avoid going away a distance.

7. When he speaks, a scholar must not shout and yell like animals and wild beasts and not raise his voice over much, but speak quietly with all creatures. When he speaks quietly, he should take care not to be so unusual as to sound arrogant and should welcome with peace all men in order that their spirits may be contented with him. He ought to judge everyone with generosity, telling what brings honour to his friend and not ever of his disgrace, and loving peace and the pursuit of peace. If he sees that his words are useful and are listened to, he speaks, but if not, he is silent. For example, he should not try to please his friend at a time when he is angry, or ask him about a vow at the time when it is made, but after his mind cools down and rests. He should not offer comfort at an hour when his friend's dead one lies before him, because he is dismayed until after the burial and likewise in other circumstances. He should not see his friend when in disgrace but turn his eyes away. He must not go back on his word,

neither add nor subtract from it except for the sake of peace or a similar reason. In general he had better not speak unless he says something wise, or in charity, and the like. He should not talk to a woman in the market place, even if she is his wife or sister or daughter.

8.   A scholar must not go about with his head in the air and outstretched neck or on tiptoe slowly like conceited women of whom it was said: 'The daughters on Zion are haughty and walk with stretched forth necks and wanton eyes mincing as they go, and making a tinkling with their feet' (Isaiah 3:16). He ought not to rush after the fashion of the crowd as the silly do, or bend down like a hunchback but keep the eyes lowered as one does when praying. In the market he ought to walk as one preoccupied by his affairs. For by the gait of a man one recognises whether he is wise and has understanding or is a silly fool. About such Solomon, in his wisdom, said: 'When he that is a fool walketh by the way, his wisdom faileth him and he saith to every one that he is a fool' (Ecclesiastes 10:3), which means that he himself proclaims that he is stupid.

9.   A scholar's dress ought to be pleasant and clean and not allowed to have a spot or grease mark. He must not dress in royal clothes of gold and purple so that every one looks at him. Neither must he dress in poor clothes which disgrace the wearer, but in comely and moderate clothes. His flesh should not be seen through them more than necessary, as it is with very fine linen that they wear in Egypt. His clothes should not trail on the ground, as with vain persons, but should reach the heel, and in the arm to the beginning of the fingers. He may not trail his prayer shawl because it looks arrogant, except on the Sabbath if he has no change of shawl. He ought not to wear shoes covered with patches in the hot weather, but in the winter it is allowed if he is a poor man. He ought not to go perfumed in the market or with scent on his garments and hair. However, if he puts perfume on his body to take away perspiration, it is allowed. He must not go out alone at night unless he has a fixed hour to go to study, in order that there may not be any suspicion.

10.   A scholar arranges his affairs wisely. He eats and drinks and he feeds the members of his household according to his means and prosperity; he should not overwork himself more than is necessary. The sages commanded that it was good manners only to eat meat when there was a desire for it as the verse says: 'Thy soul longeth to eat flesh' (Deuteronomy

12:20). It was sufficient for a healthy person to eat flesh on the eve of each Sabbath. If he was very rich, he could have meat every day. The sages advised and said that a man ought always to eat less than he could afford according to his means and dress himself adequately, but in these matters he should be specially generous to his wife and children.

11. The way of sensible people is that a man should firstly decide on work to make himself a breadwinner, then buy a dwelling house and after that take a wife, as the verse states: 'What man is he that hath planted a vineyard and hath not eaten of it? And what man is there that hath betrothed a wife, and hath not taken her?' (Deuteronomy 20:6,7). But fools first take a wife and after, if they have enough money, buy a house and then at the end of their days return to seek a living or depend on charity. When pronouncing curses this is reversed. 'A wife thou shalt betroth, a house thou shalt build and a vineyard thou shalt plant', which is to say, your affairs shall be in reverse so that you shall not prosper in your ways. In connection with blessings, the verse says: 'David behaved himself wisely in all his ways; and the Lord was with him' (I Samuel 18:14).

12. A man is forbidden to renounce or make Holy all his riches and be a burden to society. He may not sell a field and buy a house, or sell a house and buy chattels and merchandise with the value of his house. He may sell goods to buy a field and, in general, his purpose should be to increase his wealth and exchange the perishable for the durable. His intention should not be to find a little temporary joy or enjoy for a while and thereby sustain great loss.

13. A scholar should conduct business in genuine good faith; his 'no' being 'no' and his 'yes', 'yes', and he should be careful in his accountability to others but not overcritical of them. He should pay quickly and not become surety or trustee or agent, or undertake obligations in business, which are not required in the Torah, so that he may stand by his word and not change it. If the law gives judgment in his favour, he should allow time, accept excuses, lend and be merciful. He must not interfere with his neighbour's business or endanger his livelihood. The general rule is that a scholar may be pursued but not be a pursuer, may be abused but not be an abuser. Of a man who observes these things and the like, the verse says: 'And the Lord said unto me, Thou art my servant, O Israel, in whom I will be glorified' (Isaiah 49:3).

Chapter 6

1.   It is in the nature of man that he should be attracted by
the beliefs and doings of neighbours and friends and behave
as the other members of the state. On this account it is
necessary for him to associate with the righteous and to dwell
among the wise always in order to learn their ways and
remove himself from evil doers who go in darkness, lest he
should learn their deeds. This is what Solomon said: 'He that
walketh with wise men shall be wise: but a companion of
fools shall be destroyed' (Proverbs 13:20). It is also said:
'Blessed is the man that walketh not in the counsel of the
ungodly' (Psalm 1:1). So if a man lives in a country whose
customs are evil and its people are not upright, he ought to
go to a place where the people are righteous and follow good
ways. If in all the countries known to him and reported to
him the people conduct themselves badly — as happens in our
times — or if he cannot go to a country of good customs
because of robbers or epidemics, he should live alone, as was
said: 'He sitteth alone and keepeth silence' (Lamentations
3:28). If the people are wicked sinners and will not let him
stay in a country unless he mixes with them and follows their
bad customs, then he must go out to caves, and thickets and
desert places and not conduct himself in the way of sinners.
As was said: 'Oh that I had in the wilderness a lodging place'
(Jeremiah 9:2).
2.   It is a positive commandment to attach oneself to the
wise and their pupils in order to learn their deeds, as was
said: 'to him shalt thou cleave' (Deuteronomy 10:20). How
is it possible to cleave to the Divine Presence? The sages
interpreted this commandment about adhering to the wise
and their pupils as meaning that a man should be careful to
marry the daughter of a scholar and give his daughter in
marriage to one, to eat and drink with scholars, to do
business with scholars and associate with them in all ways, as
the verse says: 'cleave unto him' (Deuteronomy 11:22). The
sages also commanded and said: 'Sit in the dust at their feet
and drink with thirst their words'.[1]
3.   It is a positive commandment for each man to love each
Israelite as himself, as the verse says: 'Thou shalt love thy
neighbour as thyself' (Leviticus 19:18). So it is mandatory to
recount praises of thy neighbour and to care for his goods as
one cares for one's own and one's own honour. He who

---

[1] Ethics of the Fathers 1.4.

honours himself in the disgrace of his friend has no share in the world to come.

4. About love of a stranger who comes to shelter under the Divine Presence,[1] there are two positive commandments. First, that he is included among neighbours; secondly, that being a stranger, the law commands: 'Love ye therefore the stranger' (Deuteronomy 10:19). The Lord commanded the love for the stranger as He commanded the love for Himself. The verse states: 'Thou shalt love the Lord thy God'; and the Holy One — blessed be He — Himself loves the stranger, as the verse states: 'He loveth the stranger' (Deuteronomy 10:18).

5. Anyone who hates an Israelite in his heart transgresses the negative command. The verse states: 'Thou shalt not hate thy brother in thine heart' (Leviticus 19:17). There are no stripes as punishment in this prohibition because no deed is done.[2] The Torah only warns against hatred in the heart. But he who strikes his brother and insults him, although it is improper to do so, has not violated the command about hatred in the heart.

6. When a man sins against another, the damaged one shall not hate him and should remain silent. As was said concerning the wicked: 'Absalom spake unto his brother Amnon neither good nor bad; for Absalom hated Amnon' (2 Samuel 13:22). But it is a duty to make it known and to say: 'Why have you done thus and thus to me and sinned against me in such a way?' For the verse states: 'Thou shalt surely rebuke thy neighbour' (Leviticus 19:17). If he repents and asks for pardon he must be forgiven, and the forgiver must not be cruel, as the verse states: 'Abraham prayed unto God' (Genesis 20:17).

7. If a man sees his friend sinning or following what is not a good path, it is his duty to restore him to what is better and make known to him that he is sinning against himself by his evil doings. As the verse states: 'Thou shalt in any wise rebuke[3] thy neighbour' (Leviticus 19:17). He who corrects his friend, whether the matter is between man and man, or between man and God, must do so between themselves; and he should speak calmly and in a gentle voice making known

---

[1] The stranger *(ger)* who has become a proselyte.

[2] Transgression of a negative command was punished with stripes, but Maimonides seems here to have required some action.

[3] The verb 'to rebuke' is repeated twice implying great emphasis. In the Greek New Testament, emphasis is given by the phrase 'verily, verily I say'.

that he speaks for his friend's good and to bring him life in the 'world to come'. If the sinner accepts, it is good; but if not, he must be admonished twice, even thrice. It is always a duty to correct even until the sinner strikes one and says, 'I will not listen'. Anyone who has the power to prevent evil and does not do so will be overtaken by the evil that he could have prevented.

8.   One who first rebukes a friend should not use harsh words to shame him, as the verse says: 'Thou shalt ... not suffer sin upon him' (Leviticus 19:17), and the sages said: 'Are we allowed to rebuke until his face changes?'. From this the Rabbis decided that it is forbidden to shame an Israelite, especially in public; although he who shames his friend is not flogged, it is a great sin. Thus the sages said that he who shames his friend in public has no share in the 'world to come'. Therefore one should be careful not to disgrace a friend in public, whether he is young or old, and should not call him by a name which is shameful or speak in front of him about something that he is ashamed of. All these matters are those which arise between a man and his neighbour. In sacred matters, if the evil-doer does not repent after secret rebuke, he must be publicly shamed and his sin spread abroad; he must be rebuked to his face, disgraced and accused until he returns to the good, even as all the prophets of Israel did with the wicked.

9.   Anyone whom his neighbour has wronged, and who does not want to rebuke or say anything, because the wrong-doer is so ignorant or distracted in mind, should forgive him in his heart and not bear a grudge or correct him. Such is the way of piety, for the Torah is not concerned with aught except hatred.

10. A man has a duty to be careful with orphans and widows because their souls are very depressed and their spirits low, even if they have plenty of money. We are warned even about the widow and orphans of a king, and the verse states: 'Ye shall not afflict any widow, or fatherless child' (Exodus 22:22). How are we to behave to them? One must speak only gently to them and treat them honourably, not pain their bodies with work or their hearts with hard words and must look after their money more carefully than one's own. Anyone who annoys them or distresses them and causes them pain or oppresses them and loses their money violates a negative commandment; how much more anyone who strikes or curses them. Flogging is not administered for

breaking this negative command, but punishment is clearly stated in the Torah: 'My wrath shall wax hot and I will kill you with the sword' (Exodus 22:24). He made a covenant with them, He who spoke and created the world, that whenever they cried out against wrong they would be answered. The verse states: 'If ... they cry at all unto me, I will surely hear their cry' (Exodus 22:23). These rules apply when a person afflicts them for his own sake; but the master who teaches them the Torah, or makes them go in the path of right, is allowed to punish. However, he ought not to conduct himself to them as he does to others, but separate them and lead them gently, with great pity and honour. Proverbs 22:23 says: 'For the Lord will plead their cause'. It is the same whether the orphan is without a father or a mother. How long are they considered to be orphans? Until they have no need to lean upon and depend upon an adult but can do what they need for themselves like other adults.

Chapter 7

1.   One who slanders his friends violates a negative commandment, as the verse says: 'Thou shalt not go up and down as a tale bearer among thy people' (Leviticus 19:16). Although flogging is not applied for this, it is a great sin which causes destruction of many souls in Israel. For this reason the next verse says: 'Neither shalt thou stand against the blood of thy neighbour'. Learn what happened to Doeg the Edomite! (1 Samuel 22:9-19).

2.   Who is a tale bearer? He who collects tales and goes from one person to another saying, 'so and so said this, and this I heard of another'; although it may be true, he makes the world desolate. There is a greater sin included in this prohibition and that is the evil tongue, the slanderer who speaks of the disgrace of his friend, even although he speaks true. If he lies, he is called the bringer of an evil name on his friend. He of the evil tongue sits and says: 'so and so did something; thus and thus were his fathers; this and that I heard about him'. He says shameful things and of him it is written: 'The Lord shall cut off all flattering lips ...' (Psalm 12:3).

3.   The sages said: 'There are three transgressions for which punishment is exacted in this world and the transgressor has no portion in the 'world to come'. These are idolatry, sexual

47

immorality, and bloodshed, but the evil tongue exceeds them all'. They also said: 'All who speak with the evil tongue are as one who denies the principles of religion'. As the verse says: 'With our tongue will we prevail; our lips are our own; who is Lord over us?' (Psalm 12:4). Further, the sages said: 'The evil tongue destroys three, the speaker, the hearer, the one spoken about, and the hearer more than the speaker'.

4.   There are some matters which are the dust that covers up slander. For example, one who tells someone to be careful or says 'be quiet about so and so, I don't want to tell what happened', or such like words. If one recounts good of his friends in the presence of his enemies, that is also the dust of slander, because it causes them to speak shamefully of him. About this, Solomon said in Proverbs 27:14: 'He that blesseth his friend with a loud voice, rising early in the morning, it shall be counted a curse to him'. In the midst of the good is brought damage. In the same way, Solomon in his wisdom said that anyone who speaks evil in the guise of a joke or frivolity, as if he were not speaking in hatred of him is: 'As the madman, who scatters fire and arrows, and death' (Proverbs 26:18). Also similar is anyone speaking with the evil tongue, deceitfully yet simply, as if he did not know that his words were evil, and when protest is made against him, he says he did not know that it was slander or that these were the deeds of so and so.

5.   It is the same if the slander is spoken before the friend or behind his back. He who starts the talk and passes it from mouth to mouth causing harm to his fellow, to body or property, or distresses him, or alarms him, that speaker has the evil tongue. If the words are spoken before three others, the matter is then publicly known and, if one of the three repeats it again, that is not slander if he did not intentionally pass on the rumour and increase it.

6.   All these are regarded as possessing evil tongues and it is forbidden to dwell in their neighbourhood, and much more to live with them and listen to their words. The decree against our fathers in the wilderness was only issued because of the evil tongue (Numbers 14:35) (story of the spies).

7.   He who takes vengeance of his fellow transgresses the negative commandment: 'Thou shalt not avenge' (Leviticus 19:18), and, although whipping is not applied, it is considered a very great evil. It is comely for man to overlook things in wordly affairs because to those who are wise everything is vain and foolish and not worthy of vengeance. What

is meant by revenge? One says to one's friend, 'lend me your axe', and he answers 'I will not'. The next day he himself has need to ask for an axe and the other answers that he will not, just as it was refused him; that is taking vengeance. When one is asked, the thing should be given in good heart with no doing as you were done by, and so on. David, in his good understanding, said: 'They have rewarded me evil for good, and hatred for my love' (Psalm 109:5).

8.   Similarly, anyone who has a grudge against an Israelite transgresses a negative commandment. As the verse says: 'Thou shalt not ... bear any grudge against the children of thy people' (Leviticus 19:18). What is to bear a grudge? Reuben said to Simeon: 'lease me this house or lend me this ox' and Simeon did not want to. After a while, Simeon came to Reuben to ask for something or to hire something from him. Reuben says to him, 'there you are, I lend it, I am not like you, I will not do as you did'. Whoever says that transgresses the negative command: 'Thou shalt not bear a grudge'. He ought to blot out the affair from his heart and not be grudging. For all the time that he remembers a grudge, it is possible that it may come to vengeance. On this account the Torah was particular about grudging, so that the evil is to be blotted out of the heart and forgotten. This is the proper advice, that makes it possible for the inhabitants of the land to live and do business with one another.

Here ends the treatise on Discernment

Treatise 3
THE STUDY OF THE TORAH

Two positive commandments are contained in this Treatise and they are:
(a) To study the Torah.
(b) To honour those who study and understand it.

Chapter 1

1.   Women, servants[1] and small children are excused from studying but the father of a little boy is obliged to teach him the Torah, as the verse says: 'And ye shall teach them your children, speaking of them' (Deuteronomy 11:19). A woman is not obliged to teach her child, for only those whose duty it is to study have a duty to teach.

2.   Just as a man has a duty to teach his child, he has a duty to teach his grandchild, as the verse says: 'Teach them thy sons, and thy sons' sons' (Deuteronomy 4:9), and not only his children and grandchildren. For it is a command that every scholar in Israel should teach those who seek learning, even although they are not his children. The verse says: 'And thou shalt teach them diligently unto thy children' (Deuteronomy 6:7). By tradition pupils are also called children. The verse in 2 Kings 2:3 says: 'And the sons of the prophets ... came forth' (meaning pupils). Why then is one commanded to teach children and grandchildren? In order to attend to one's children before grandchildren, and grandchildren before the children of one's friends.

3.   It is a duty to hire a teacher to teach one's child but it is not a duty to teach a friend's child for nothing. Anyone not taught by his father must educate himself when he becomes mature. The verse in Deuteronomy 5:1 says: 'That ye may learn them, and keep, and do them'. Generally speaking, one finds that learning leads to action, for study brings forth action,[2] but action does not lead to learning.

---

[1] See Exodus 21:1 and Leviticus 25:39. There was no slavery in Israel but a man could bind himself to work for another because of poverty or to make restitution for a crime, such as theft.

[2] During the Hadrianic persecutions when both study and religious duties were forbidden, it was decided that study should have first place as being less perilous than overt religious action.

4.   If one is anxious to study Torah and has a son studying, one's own study comes before the son's. If the son is the cleverer and the more able to understand what he learns, the son comes first. However, although the son comes first, one may not give up study because the same command to teach the son applies to teaching oneself.

5.   A man should study first and then marry. If he marries first, his mind is not free to study, but if he finds his desire overcomes him and his mind is not free, he should marry and study Torah afterwards.

6.   At what age is it a father's duty to teach the Torah? When the child begins to speak, he should be taught two verses: 'Moses commanded us a law' (Deuteronomy 33:4) and 'Hear, O Israel' (Deuteronomy 6:4). After that the child should be taught little by little, verse by verse, according to his development, until he is six or seven years old, and then he should be put under a children's teacher.

7.   If it is the custom in the region to hire a children's teacher, this must be done, and it is a duty to pay until the child can read the whole written law.[1] In a place where it is customary to teach the written Torah for reward, it is permitted to take pay, but it is forbidden to teach the oral tradition for pay. The verse says: 'Behold, I have taught you statutes and judgments, even as the Lord my God commanded me' (Deuteronomy 4:5), meaning, 'what I learned for nothing so you must teach for nothing what came from me', likewise, 'when you teach the next generations, teach them for nothing as you were taught by me'. If no man can be found to teach without payment, teaching must be paid for, as the verse says: 'Buy the truth' (Proverbs 23:23). Can he therefore teach for nothing? The same verse says: 'sell it not'. Learn from this that it is forbidden to teach the oral law for hire although your teacher did so.

8.   Every Israelite has a duty to study whether he is poor or rich, whether healthy or suffering, whether young or very old and in failing strength, even if he is poor and supported by charity or begs from door to door. Even if he is a married man with a wife and children, it is a duty to set aside time to study, day and night, as the verse says: 'Thou shalt meditate therein day and night' (Joshua 1:8).

9.   Among the great scholars of Israel some were hewers of

---

[1] Pentateuch is written law. Oral law is Mishnah and Talmud which were only written down after the destruction of Jerusalem and the Temple.

wood and drawers of water, and some were blind, but in spite of that they studied by day and night. They were of those who passed on the verbal tradition from mouth to mouth from Moses our teacher.[1]

10. For how long is it a duty to study the Law? To the day of death. The verse says: 'Lest they depart from thy heart all the days of thy life' (Deuteronomy 4:9). When one does not study one forgets.

11. It is a duty to divide the time for study into three parts, one third for the written word, one third for the oral tradition and one third to understand things completely, and deduce one from another, and to compare one thing with another, and to know the rules by which the Torah is expounded until one grasps the principle of the rules and knows which things are forbidden, which are permitted and which are learned by tradition. This study is known as *Gemara*.

12. To give an example, an artisan busies himself with his work for three hours each day and spends nine hours in study. Of the nine hours, for three he ought to study the written law, for three the oral law and for three investigate his knowledge and understanding of matters one from another. Traditional matters are included in the Holy Writ and their explanations are in the oral law. The subjects relating to the *Pardes* are in the *Gemara* generally. When do these rules apply? When a man begins to study. When he has acquired knowledge he has no need to study the Holy Writ or to busy himself with the oral tradition, and he should then read the written law and oral law at fixed times (so that he may not forget any of the laws of the Torah) and turn every day to the *Gemara* according to the capacity of his heart and the equanimity of his mind.

13. A woman who studies the Torah has a reward but not the reward of a man because she is not commanded to do it. One who does something which is not mandatory has not the reward of one who obeys a command, but a smaller reward. Although she has a reward, the sages commanded that a man should not teach his daughter the Torah because most women have not the capacity to apply themselves to learning; they change the matters of the Torah into nonsense because of their poor understanding. The sages said of anyone who

---

[1] The tradition of the Elders was the unwritten laws given to Moses on Mount Sinai and handed down verbally, for example, laws about washing the hands, etc.

taught his daughter the Torah that it was as if he taught indecency and, according to tradition, this applies to teaching of the oral law. As regards the written Torah, he should not start to teach her at all, but, if he does, there is no impropriety in that.

Chapter 2

1.   We appoint teachers for the young in every province, district and city. In a city in which there is no school the inhabitants are ostracised until they appoint children's teachers and, if it is not done, the city is ostracised for the world cannot be preserved without the utterance of school children.[1]

2.   Children should be collected to be taught when they are six or seven years old, depending upon their understanding and the strength of their bodies. Under six years, they should not be enrolled. The teacher may punish them to instil awe in them but he may not strike them in enmity or cruelty. He may, therefore, not whip them with a scourge or a stick but with a little strap. He should instruct them all day and some of the night to accustom them to learn by day and night. They should not be idle except on the evenings of Sabbath and the festivals, and on festive days. On the Sabbath there is no new lesson, only repetitions. Children should not be rendered idle, even for the sake of building a temple.

3.   A teacher who leaves the children and goes out or undertakes other work with them, or becomes lazy in teaching, is as one of whom the verse says: 'Cursed be he that doeth the work of the Lord deceitfully' (Jeremiah 48:10). So it is only proper to appoint a teacher who is God-fearing, as well as proficient in reading, and strict.

4.   He who does not have a wife may not instruct little children because of the mothers who bring them, and a woman may not teach little children because of the fathers who come along with them.

5.   Twenty-five children may learn from one teacher. If there are more than twenty-five and up to forty, an assistant should be appointed to help in the teaching. If there are more than forty, two children's teachers are needed.

6.   A school child may be transferred from one teacher to another who is more diligent. This is done when there are two teachers in a city and no river divides them. But children

[1] Implying repeated recitations of the Law in classes.

should not be transferred between cities, or when a river divides one side of a city from the other, unless there is a good ford through the river or a bridge that will not break easily.

7.   If a man in a particular neighbourhood wishes to become a teacher, his neighbours cannot prevent him. Even if he opens a school in the same courtyard as another teacher either to teach other children or to take pupils away from the other, he cannot be prevented, as the verse says: 'The Lord is well pleased for his righteousness' sake; he will magnify the law, and make it honourable' (Isaiah 42:21).

Chapter 3

1.   Israel was crowned with three crowns — the crown of the Torah, the crown of the priesthood and the crown of kingship. The crown of the priesthood was awarded to Aaron. As the verse says: 'And he shall have it, and his seed after him, even the covenant of an everlasting priest-hood' (Numbers 25:13). The crown of kingship was awarded to David. As the verse says: 'His seed shall endure for ever, and his throne as the sun before me' (Psalm 89:36). The crown of the Torah, behold, it lies and is available for every Israelite. As the verse says: 'Moses commanded us a law, even the inheritance of the congregation of Jacob' (Deuteronomy 33:4). All who wish may come and take it up. If you will say that the others are greater than the crown of the Torah, behold, it is said: 'By me kings reign, and princes decree justice. By me princes rule, and nobles, ...' (Proverbs 8:15, 16). Learn from this that the crown of the Torah is greater than the two others.[1]

2.   The sages stated that an illegitimate scholar has precedence over an illiterate priest. As the verse says: 'She (wisdom) is more precious than rubies' (Proverbs 3:15), meaning that wisdom was more precious than the High Priest who enters the innermost part of the Temple.[2]

3.   There is not one of all the commandments in the Torah which compares with the commandment to study the Law, because study leads to practice. Study, therefore, comes before practice.

[1] In the second century Simeon Ben Yochai added a fourth, namely 'the crown of a good name', which he thought excelled them all. (Ethics of the Fathers, 4:17).

[2] The High Priest was allowed to enter the Holy of Holies only once a year on the Day of Atonement to pray for the people of Israel.

4.   If one is confronted with the choice between fulfilling a commandment and studying the Torah and it is possible for another to fulfil the action, one should not interrupt one's studies, but if that is not possible, the deed should be done and study resumed.

5.   The first question asked in the judgment of a man is 'Have you studied?' and after that he is asked about other deeds. The wise men stated: 'Let a man always study the Torah whether for its own sake or not; even if it is not at first for its own sake, the study leads on to that'.

6.   Anyone who sets his heart to fulfil this duty properly and to be crowned with the crown of the Torah must not let his mind be occupied with other matters, nor set his heart on acquiring the Torah and riches and fame together. The way to the Torah is a 'morsel of bread and salt that thou shalt eat and a measure of water that thou shalt drink, thou shalt sleep on the ground and have a hard life when thou toilest in the Torah'. It is not upon you to finish it, nor are you free to neglect it, but if you increase the study the reward increases. The reward is according to the hardship.

7.   Perhaps you may say, 'I will gather money and then return to study; I will obtain what I need and then turn from business to study'. If you think that, you will never be worthy of the crown of the Torah. You should make the Torah essential and your work temporal and do not say, 'When I am free I shall study'. Perhaps you will not be free.

8.   In Deuteronomy 30:12,13, it is written: 'It (the command) is not in heaven ... neither is it beyond the sea'. 'It is not in heaven' means that it is not found in the arrogant nor found in those who travel overseas. The sages stated: 'All those who busy themselves in commerce do not become wise', and they commanded: 'Deal less in business but busy yourself with the study of the Torah'.

9.   The words of the Torah are compared with water. The verse says: 'Ho, everyone that thirsteth come ye to the waters' (Isaiah 55:1), which teaches you that, as waters do not collect in steep places but trickle down into flats, so in like manner the words of the Torah are not found in the haughty spirit or proud heart, but in the lowly and subdued spirit which mixes with the dust at the feet of the sages, removes the desires and pleasures of the day from his heart, does such little work each day as is needed for living and spends the rest of his days and nights in study.

10.   Anyone who sets his heart on being occupied with

Torah and does not work but depends upon charity, profanes the Holy Name, shames the Torah and puts out the light of religion. He brings evil to himself and removes his life from the world to come because it is forbidden to derive worldly benefit from the Torah in this world. The ancient fathers stated: 'One who makes benefit from the words of the Torah takes his life out of the world', and further they commanded: 'Thou shalt not make of it a garland to magnify thyself, nor a spade to dig with'. Yet again, they commanded: 'Love work and hate high office'. For one who studies without work, the end is idleness and leads to sin. The end of such a man will be that he will rob people.

11. There is great merit to him who earns his living by the work of his hands, as was the way of the ancient pious men of the past. Such a man is worthy of all honour and good in this world and in the world to come. As the verse says: 'For thou shalt eat the labour of thine hands: happy shalt thou be and it shall be well with thee' (Psalm 128:2). You will be happy in this world and it will be well with you in the world to come, which is altogether good.

12. The words of the Torah do not survive in one who is slack about them, and not with those who study in luxury and indulge in food and drinking, but with one who sacrifices himself for them and who leads a hard life always and does not allow his eyes to sleep nor his eyelids to slumber. The sages said in a parable: 'This is the Law, when a man dieth in a tent' (Numbers 19:14). The Law will not remain with him unless he sacrifices himself in the tents of the wise. As Solomon in his wisdom said: 'If thou faint in the day of adversity, thy strength is small' (Proverbs 24:10). He also said: 'My wisdom remained with me' (Ecclesiastes 2:9) — 'the wisdom, which I learned by real effort, stood by me'. The sages said: 'There is a covenant that all who toil in study of the Torah in the school of *Midrash* (see glossary) will not easily forget it, and he who toils with Torah in secret shall become wise'. As the verse says: 'with the lowly is wisdom' (Proverbs 11:2). He who reads aloud when studying will retain it, but he who reads in a whisper forgets quickly.

13. Although it is commanded to study both by day and by night, man learns most at night. So anyone who wishes to be worthy of the crown of the Torah should take care of his nights, not to waste any of them in sleeping, eating, drinking and talking, and so on, but in studying Torah and words of wisdom. The sages said: 'The song of the Torah cannot be

heard except at night'. As the verse says: 'Arise, cry out in the night' (Lamentations 2:19). He who pursues the study of the Torah by night has a thread of loving kindness drawn upon himself by day. As the verse says: 'Yet the Lord will command his loving kindness in the day time, and in the night His song shall be with me, and my prayer unto the God of my life' (Psalm 42:8). Every house in which the words of the Torah are not heard in the night time will be consumed with fire. The verse says: 'All darkness shall be hid in his secret places: a fire not blown shall consume him' (Job 20:26), and 'Because he hath despised the word of the Lord, and hath broken his commandment' (Numbers 15:31). Likewise he who has the chance to busy himself with learning and does not do so, or who has studied and become proficient in the Torah and abandons his study for the sake of the vanities of the world, he is of those 'who despise the word of the Lord'. The sages said: 'Anyone who neglects the Torah on account of riches will in the end abandon it on account of poverty, but whoever sticks to learning in poverty will in the end study in wealth'. This is clearly stated in the Torah where it says: 'Because thou servest not the Lord thy God with joyfulness, and with gladness of heart, for the abundance of all things: therefore shalt thou serve thine enemies' (Deuteronomy 28:47), and further, 'that He might humble thee and that He might prove thee to do thee good at thy latter end' (Deuteronomy 8:16).

Chapter 4

1.   Instruction in Torah should not be given except to suitable well behaved pupils, and to the simple minded. If one has followed a path which is not good, one must be brought back to the better way, conducted in the path of righteousness and examined, and after that one may be admitted to the school of instruction and be taught. The sages said: 'He who instructs one who is unfit is like throwing a stone to Hermes'. The verse in Proverbs 26:8 says: 'As he that bindeth a stone in a sling, so is he that giveth honour to a fool'. There is no glory except in the Torah, as the verse says: 'The wise shall inherit glory' (Proverbs 3:35). Likewise, we must not learn from a rabbi who does not follow the good way although he be a great scholar and all people need him, until he returns to better ways. The verse says: 'For the priest's lips should keep knowledge, and they should seek the

law at his mouth: for he is the messenger of the Lord of hosts' (Malachi 2:7). The sages said that if a teacher arises who is like a messenger of the Lord of Hosts, then they should seek the Law from his mouth but, if he is not, they shall not seek the Law from him.

2.   How does one teach? The rabbi sits at the head and the pupils surround him like a crown, in order that all may see him and hear his words. The teacher does not sit on a seat and the pupils on the ground, but either all sit on the ground or all on seats. Originally the teacher sat and the pupils stood. From before the destruction of the second Temple it was customary to teach with the pupils seated.

3.   The teacher may speak directly to the pupils or through an interpreter. The interpreter stands between the teacher and the pupils, and the teacher speaks to the interpreter who repeats it to the pupils. When the pupils ask questions, they ask the interpreter and he asks the teacher who answers the interpreter, and the interpreter answers the questioner. The teacher must not raise his voice above that of the interpreter, and the interpreter may not raise his voice (when the question is asked) above that of the teacher. The interpreter is not allowed to diminish, or to add, or to change anything unless the interpreter is the teacher's father or his master. The teacher says to the interpreter: 'Thus I was taught by my rabbi or by my father, my teacher'. But when the interpreter repeats these words to the audience he may give the name of the wise man and mention the name of the father of the rabbi or his master, saying: 'Thus said such and such a rabbi', although the teacher himself did not mention the scholar's name. For it is forbidden to mention by name one's master or one's father.[1]

4.   When a rabbi is teaching and the pupils do not understand, he must not be vexed with them and be agitated. he must return and repeat the matter over and over again until they understand the significance of the passage. Likewise, a disciple may not say 'I understand' when he does not but must ask again, even many times. And if the teacher becomes angry with him and irritated, he may say to him: 'My master, this is Torah and I have to learn it, my mind is short of understanding'.

5.   A disciple should not feel ashamed before his fellows who learned the first or second time and he did not after many times. For if he is ashamed of that, he will enter and

---

[1] Considered grave discourtesy.

leave the Midrash school without learning anything. Because of this, the sages of old said: 'One who is ashamed cannot learn and the irritable cannot teach'. When do these sayings apply? When the pupils do not understand the subject on account of its profundity or because of their lack of intelligence. However, if the teacher realises that they are being lazy about the words of the Torah and slack so that they do not understand, he may be angry and shame them to stimulate them. On this matter, the sages said: 'Cast bitterness at the pupils'. It is therefore not desirable for the teacher to be frivolous before pupils, and to laugh with them and eat and drink with them, so that they may hold him in awe and learn quickly.

6.　　Questions may not be asked of the teacher as soon as he enters the school but must wait until his mind has settled down. A student may not ask a question when he comes in but must wait until he sits down and rests. Two pupils may not ask at the same time and they may not ask about a matter which is not relevant to the subject being dealt with, lest the rabbi be put to shame. The teacher may perplex the students with the questions to stimulate them and to find out whether they are remembering what he has taught them or not. Needless to say, he is allowed to ask them something not under discussion to make them alert.

7.　　No questions may be asked nor answers given when standing, and not from raised places, from a distance or behind the elders. The teacher may only be asked questions about relevant matters and in seriousness, and only three questions are allowed about the same subject.

8.　　If two pupils ask questions and one is about the subject in hand and the other not relevant, the first has priority. In a matter of practice and theory, practice has precedence; in a matter of law and homiletics, law has precedence; in homiletics and folklore, the latter gives way to homiletics; attention being paid always from minor to major.[1] If there are two questioners, one a scholar and the other a pupil, the scholar has precedence. If they are a pupil and an illiterate person, the pupil has priority. If both are scholars or both are pupils or illiterate persons, and if both ask about the same passage or the same answers, or there are two questions about the same practice, the interpreter is permitted to deal with it.

9.　　One is not allowed to sleep in the Midrash school and

[1] This paragraph quotes two of the 13 exegetical principles of the Law — see Prayer Book.

all who slumber there have their wisdom in tatters. Solomon in his wisdom said: 'drowsiness shall clothe a man in rags' (Proverbs 23:21). Conversations are not allowed in the school of Midrash, only the words of Torah. Even if someone sneezes, one may not wish him health in the Midrash school and it is needless to mention other matters. The school of Midrash is more holy than the synagogue.

Chapter 5

1. Just as a man is commanded to honour and revere his father, so it is his duty to honour his teacher and to fear him more than his father. For his father brings him into the life of this world but it is his rabbi who teaches him wisdom and brings him to life in the world to come. If he sees something lost by his father and his rabbi, his rabbi's loss comes before his father's. If his father and his rabbi are carrying loads, he helps the rabbi and after that his father. If father and rabbi are captured, the rabbi should be ransomed first and after that his father. If his father is a scholar, he is ransomed first, even if his father is not so learned as the rabbi, and his lost possessions should be brought back first and the rabbi's afterwards. There is no greater honour than that due to a rabbi and no greater reverence than that of the teacher. Because of this, it was said by the sages: 'Fear your master as you fear Heaven'. So they said: 'Whoever disputes with his rabbi it is as if he disputes with the *Shechinah*. As the verse says: 'They strove against the Lord' (Numbers 26:9). When someone quarrels with his rabbi, it is as if he quarrelled with the *Shechinah*. As the verse says: 'Because the children of Israel strove with the Lord, and He was sanctified in them' (Numbers 20:13). Anyone who complains of his teacher, it is as if he spoke ill against the Lord. As the verse says: 'Your murmerings are not against us but against the Lord' (Exodus 16:8). Anyone who has suspicions about a rabbi, it is as if he suspects the *Shechinah*. As the verse says: 'And the people spake against God and against Moses' (Numbers 21:5).
2. Who is thought to be in opposition to his master? He who sets up a school and settles down and gives instruction and teaches without permission from his master who is still alive, and even if he is in another district. It is forbidden even to instruct in front of the teacher, and anyone who gives a

decision on law in the presence of his rabbi deserves death.
3. If there are twelve miles distance between a man and
his rabbi and someone asks him a question about the Law, he
is allowed to answer. To guard against a forbidden act, it is
permissible to answer in the teacher's presence. For example,
if someone sees a man doing something forbidden who does
not know that it is forbidden, or because of wickedness, it is
a duty to prevent him and say to the doer, 'that is forbidden',
even in the presence of the rabbi although the rabbi did not
give him permission. For all cases of profanation, one is not
in duty bound to honour the teacher. When does this apply?
When it is an occasional happening. However, if a man
appoints himself to teach and answer questions, that is
forbidden even if he and his rabbi are worlds apart in
distance. That holds until his rabbi dies or has given permission. Not everyone whose rabbi has died has permission
to establish himself to teach Torah, but only if he is a pupil
who is fully qualified to teach.
4. A student who is not qualified to teach and who still
instructs is certainly wicked, foolish and conceited. Of such,
the verse says: 'For she hath cast down many wounded;
yea many strong men have been slain by her' (Proverbs
7:26).[1] Similarly, a scholar, who has reached the rank of an
instructor and does not teach, surely withholds the Torah
and puts stumbling blocks before the blind, as the above
verse says. They are students who have not studied Torah as
much as is necessary and want to advance themselves among
the illiterate or among their own people, and push themselves
forward and sit in judgment to instruct Israel. They increase
divisions and lay waste the world, and put out the lamp of
the Torah and ruin the vineyard of the Lord of Hosts.
Solomon in his wisdom said of them: 'Take us the foxes, the
little foxes, that spoil the vines' (Song of Songs 2:15).
5. It is forbidden for a pupil to call his rabbi by his name,
even in his absence, but he may use a title by which he is
recognised. A pupil should not mention the teacher's name in
his presence or even the name of someone of the same name
as his teacher, just as he does with his father's name. He must
refer to him by title even after death. The pupil may not
greet his rabbi or return greetings to him in the way he greets
and replies to his friends. He should bow to him and speak
with reverence and respect, and say: 'Peace to thee, my

[1] She here means harlot, the symbol of the wicked, foolish,
conceited one.

master'. If his rabbi greets him, he should reply: 'Peace to thee, my master and teacher'.

6.   He should not remove his phylacteries in the presence of his rabbi and should not recline but sit as if in the presence of a king. He should not pray in front of his master, nor behind his back, nor at his side. Needless to say, he may not walk beside him but must keep behind him, but not directly behind him; there he may pray. He should not enter the bath house with his master. He may not sit in his master's seat, nor compromise his opinions, nor contradict them. He ought not to sit down in his master's presence until told to do so, nor stand up in his presence until told to stand or has permission to stand. When he leaves his rabbi, he must not turn his back but must retreat facing him.

7.   He is obliged to rise if he sees his rabbi coming, as far as his eyes can see, and not until the rabbi disappears and his form cannot be seen may he sit down. It is a duty to visit one's rabbi on the festivals.

8.   No special honour should be paid to a student in the presence of his rabbi unless his rabbi was in the habit of honouring him. All the work which a servant does for his master, the pupil does for his rabbi. If he is in a place where he is not known and has no phylacteries and fears that he will be taken for a servant (slave), he is not obliged to fasten on or loosen his masters' shoes. Any teacher who prevents his pupil from serving him deprives him of loving kindness, and severs his fear of Heaven. A pupil who cheapens anything about the honour of his rabbi causes the *Shechinah* to depart from Israel.

9.   If a pupil sees a rabbi doing something wrong, he should say to him: 'Our master you taught us this and thus'. Anytime he quotes what he heard in his presence, he must say: 'Thus our teacher taught us master'. He may not repeat anything that he did not hear from his teacher without giving the name of the person from whom he heard it. When a rabbi dies, as a sign of mourning a pupil rends his garment until his chest is exposed and should never mend it. When does this apply? For his distinguished master from whom he learned most of his wisdom. But if he did not learn such wisdom, then he is no more to him than a fellow student and he is not obliged to give honour in these ways. On his teacher's death he must rend his garments as he rends it for all whose death he mourns. Even if he only learned one thing, whether small or great, he must stand up before him and rend his garment.

10. No scholar of mature intelligence gives an opinion in front of someone who is greater in wisdom than he is, even although he has learned nothing from him.

11. The distinguished rabbi who wishes to forego the honours associated with these matters, or even one of them, for all his students, or even just one of them, is allowed to do so. However, a disciple is obliged to honour even at times when he forgoes all honour.

12. Just as the pupils have a duty to honour the rabbi, so the rabbi has need to honour and attract them. The sages said: 'Let the honour of your students be cherished like your own'. For one must take care of the students and love them like one's children, for the students are the sons of delight in this world and in the world to come.

13. Pupils add to the master's wisdom and broaden his heart. The sages said: 'Much wisdom have I learned from my masters, more from my friends, but most from my pupils'. Even as a small twig kindles a great fire so a little pupil stimulates the rabbi and there goes out from his questions marvellous wisdom.

Chapter 6

1. It is a positive command to honour every scholar, even although he is not one's teacher. The verse says: 'Thou shalt rise up before the hoary head, and honour the face of the old man' (Leviticus 19:32). 'Old' implies a man who has acquired wisdom. At what distance must one stand up in his presence? From the time when he is four cubits distant from one as he comes until he disappears from view.

2. It is not necessary to stand up before him in the bath house or privy, for it was said: 'Thou shalt rise up and honour', implying where there is honour. An artisan is not obliged to stand up before scholars if he is busy at work, for the saying 'Thou shalt rise up and honour' means that no financial loss is to be incurred. Where do we learn that we must not close the eyes so as not to see a sage and rise before him? In the verse: 'Thou shalt ... and fear they God' (Leviticus 19:32). Learn that this means that of everything concerning the heart it is said: 'Thou shalt fear thy God'.

3. A scholar is not allowed to trouble people and to draw attention to himself, expecting them to stand up before him. He should go by a short-cut and intend that they should not

see him, in order not to trouble them to stand up. The wise men made detours when walking, going by outer paths where those who knew them were not there to be troubled.

4.   A rider is the same as one on foot, and just as one stands up to one walking past, so one stands up for the rider.

5.   When three are walking together, the teacher shall be in the middle, the elder disciple on the right and the younger on his left side.

6.   If one sees a scholar one does not rise until he is within four cubits distance, and as soon as he passes, one may sit down. If one sees the head of the *Beth Din,* one rises as soon as one sees him from a distance and does not sit down until he has passed away four cubits. If one sees a president, one stands all the time that he can be seen and does not sit down until the president has taken his place or has passed out of sight. A president who renounces such deference is allowed to do so. When a president enters (an assembly) everyone stands and remains standing until he bids them be seated. When the head of the *Beth Din* enters the court, two rows are formed and everyone stands thus until he passes and takes his seat; then all sit down in their places.

7.   When a sage enters all who are within four cubits stand and sit down one after the other until he sits in place. When the children and pupils of the wise man are needed by the people, they have precedence over heads of the community and take their places. It is not an honour for scholars to enter last. If a scholar leaves for some reason, he returns to his place. When the disciples of the sages have enough understanding, they are seated facing their fathers in the audience. If they do not, they face the people.

8.   A pupil who studies continually with his teacher is not required to stand up before him except in the morning and evening, so that his honour should not appear greater than that of Heaven.

9.   If a man is distinguished by great old age, although not a sage, people rise up before him. Even a young sage stands up before an old man of great age, but he does not need to rise to his full height but only enough to give honour. Even an aged non-Jew should be honoured with a greeting and support by the hand. The verse says: 'Thou shalt rise up before the hoary head'. (Leviticus 19:32). Traditionally that means before all grey heads.

10.   Scholars do not go out themselves to do community work in building, and digging and the like, in order that they

may not be embarrassed by illiterate people. They are not taxed to build ramparts, repair gates, pay for the watchmen and the like, nor do they contribute to the royal presentations. They are not expected to pay taxes, whether fixed for the community or individuals. The verse says: 'Yea though they have hired themselves among the nations, now will I gather them back and they shall sorrow a little for the burden of taxes of the king of princes' (Hosea 8:10).[1] If a scholar has merchandise to sell he may sell first and we do not allow others to sell until he sells. In the same way, if he has a court case, and he stands among many others with cases, he is given priority and a seat.

11. It is a grave sin to disgrace a scholar or hate him. Jerusalem was not destroyed until the scholars were disgraced. As the verse says: 'But they mocked the messengers of God and despised His words, and misused His prophets' (2 Chronicles 36:16), which means that they despised the teachers of His word. The Torah says: 'If ye shall despise my statutes ... ye break my covenants' (Leviticus 26:15). Anyone who despises scholars has no share in the world to come; he is of those who 'despised the word of the Lord' (Numbers 15:31).

12. One who disgraces scholars has no share in the world to come. If there are witnesses that he made despising remarks, he is liable to be excommunicated by the *Beth Din* in public and be fined a gold pound in every case and it is given to a scholar. Whoever insults a scholar verbally, even after the death of the scholar, is excommunicated by the *Beth Din* but is released when he repents. But if the scholar is still alive, it cannot be reversed until the scholar is pacified. Similarly, a scholar may excommunicate anyone who is disrespectful and there is no need for witnesses or a warning to be given; and that is not reversed until he has pacified the scholar. If the scholar dies, three men may release him of excommunication. However, if the scholar wishes to excuse and not excommunicate, he may do so.

13. If a teacher pronounces excommunication in defence of his honour, all his disciples in the region must conform. But if a disciple excommunicates for his own honour, his teacher does not need to follow but the people must follow it. In this way, if a president excommunicates, all Israel must act likewise. Excommunication by all Israel does not involve the

[1] A verse accepted as very difficult of interpretation by commentators.

president. One excommunicated in his own community is ex-communicated in every other community, but one excom-municated in a community where he is a stranger is not excommunicated in his own community.

14. How does this apply? To someone who has been ostra-cised because he scorned scholars. But if he was ostracised because of some other matter (which caused that penalty), even when it was applied by the least important person in Israel, it was required that the president and all Israel conformed until repentance was made for the thing for which ostracism was pronounced, and then release was given. Ostracism was applied for twenty-four offences, and applied both to men and women. The following are offenders.

(1) One who disgraces a wise man even after his death.
(2) One who scorns a summons of the court.
(3) One who calls a fellow man a slave.
(4) One who refuses to appear in court when sum-moned.
(5) One who scoffs at the words of a scribe and, need-less to say, the words of Torah.
(6) One who disobeys the decision of the court; he is ostracised until he complies.
(7) One who keeps something dangerous, for example, a vicious dog or an unstable ladder; the owner is ostracised until he removed the danger.
(8) One who sells land to idolaters; he is banned until he accepts all obligations which may come upon an Israelite from an idolater whose land is next to his.
(9) One who testifies against an Israelite in an idola-ter's court of law, and receives money when it is contrary to Israeli law; he is ostracised until he makes redress.
(10) A priest who is a slaughterer, and who does not separate the portions and give them to another priest; he is outlawed until he makes restitution.
(11) One who profanes the second day of a festival when in exile, even although it is only a custom there.
(12) One who works on the eve of Passover after mid-day.
(13) One who takes the name of Heaven in vain or swears by it foolishly.
(14) One who leads the crowds to blaspheme the Holy Name.

(15) Those who lead the people to eat holy food outside the appointed place (the Temple).

(16) One who calculates years and fixed months outside
the land of Israel.

(17) One who causes the blind to stumble.

(18) One who prevents the people from performing a
commandment.

(19) A butcher who sells non-kosher meat underhand-
edly.

(20) A butcher who has not had his knife examined for
sharpness before a rabbi.

(21) One who exposes oneself indecently.

(22) A man who divorces his wife and makes a partner-
ship or trades with her and they depend on one
another; when brought to court, they should be
ostracised.

(23) A scholar with an evil reputation.

(24) One who pronounces excommunication on someone who does not deserve it.

Chapter 7

1.   A sage who has grown old in wisdom or a prince or head
of the *Beth Din* who does something unseemly is never ostracised in public unless he has done as Jeroboam, son of Nebat,
and his friend did, (I Kings 11:26). But, if he has committed
other sins, he is lashed in secret. The verse says: 'Therefore
shalt thou fall in the day, and the prophet also shall fall with
thee in the night' (Hosiah 4:5), implying should he fall,
cover it as if by night. He should be told 'for honour's sake
stay at home'. In the same way, when a scholar deserves
punishment, it is forbidden for the court to rush to ostracise
him in a hurry, but rather to avoid it and then turn away
from it. The pious sages prided themselves that they had
never ostracised a disciple, although they could be assigned to
take part if stripes were deserved, and even to take part in the
beating of a rebel.[1]

2.   How is excommunication pronounced? Someone says:
'So and so must be banished'. When this is said to his face,
someone says: 'This man must be excommunicated'. Then

[1] A rebel was beaten until he accepted the sentence of the *Beth
Din.*

the excommunicator says: 'So and so is excommunicated'; he is cursed, and the excommunication falls on him.

3. And how is the ostracism or excommunication removed? He is told: 'You are free and forgiven'. If the release is not given in his presence, someone tells him that he is free and pardoned.

4. What is the custom for the behaviour of the banned person himself and of others towards him? The banned one may not shave or wash as a mourner all the time of the ban and he may not be counted among the three who offer grace after meals. He may not be considered for the *minyan* or group of ten adults required for certain matters. No one may sit within four cubits of him. He may instruct others and they may instruct him, he may be hired and may hire. If he dies during the ban, the court sends and puts a stone on his coffin as if to say that they stone him because he separated himself from the community. Needless to say, he is not mourned and his hearse is not followed.

5. Punishment is heavier than this if he is excommunicated and not allowed to instruct others or to be instructed but studies alone in order not to forget his learning. Also, he may not be hired or hire others, and none may do business with him or make contact with him except for necessities of life.

6. Anyone who remains banned for thirty days and does not ask for release is sentenced again. If again he remains for thirty days without asking for release, he is excommunicated.

7. How many are needed to release the ban or excommunication? Three, even the uneducated. A single expert may annul the ban or excommunication by himself and a pupil may give release in place of a rabbi.

8. If three have pronounced a ban and gone away, and the offender repents of the thing which caused the ban, three others may come and release him.

9. If a banned one does not know who imposed the sentence, he should go to the president who may release him.

10. A conditional curse, even of one's own, needs to be annulled. A scholar who binds himself with such a ban, even on another's advice in a matter which merits a ban can release himself.

11. Anyone who dreams that he was ostracised and remembers who pronounced it must have ten men versed in law to release him. If he cannot find them, he must take pains to look for them for a mile. If he still cannot find them, he may

be released by ten men who study the Mishnah: if such cannot be found, then ten who can read Torah; failing them, ten men who cannot read. If he cannot find nearly ten adults to release him, three will do.

12. Anyone present when excommunicated must be released to his face. If he was excommunicated in his absence, release may be made either in his presence or not. Between a ban and its annulment, no time is fixed. The ban and the release may be but a minute apart if the excommunicated one repents. If the *Beth Din* decides to leave the excommunication, it may be left for years, according to the seriousness of the offence. If the *Beth Din* excommunicates first one and then another who eats or drinks with him or stands within four cubits of him, the purpose of the sentence is to punish and to build a fence round the Torah which the sinful cannot break through.

Although a scholar is allowed to excommunicate someone who has dishonoured him, it is not praiseworthy for him to do so. He should turn his ears from the talk of the illiterate and not take it to heart. Solomon in his wisdom said: 'Take no heed unto all words that are spoken' (Ecclesiastes 7:21). This was the way of the early pious men who when maligned, made no reply but excused and pardoned. The great scholars prided themselves on agreeable conduct and said that they had never ostracised or excommunicated anyone for the sake of their honour. Such is the path which the scholars should follow. When does it apply? When they are shamed and reviled secretly. But a scholar who is abused and reviled in public is forbidden to forgive offences against his honour and, if he does so, he is punished for it because it is a disgrace to the Torah. He must avenge it and treat it like a snake until pardon is sought. Then he should forgive.

Here ends the treatise on the study of the Torah.

Treatise 4
IDOLATRY

Fifty-one commandments, two positive and forty-nine negative, are enumerated here. They are:

1. Not to follow idolaters (worshippers of the stars).
2. Not to follow evil thoughts and sights of the eyes.
3. Not to blaspheme.
4. Not to worship idols in the customary way.
5. Not to bow down to them.
6. Not to make a graven image for oneself.
7. Not to make a graven image for another.
8. Not to make any image even for its beauty.
9. Not to entice others to serve it.
10. To burn an idolatrous city.
11. Not to rebuild it.
12. Not to benefit from any of its wealth.
13. Not to entice anyone to serve an idol.
14. Not to love an enticer.
15. Not to stop hating an idolater.
16. Not to save him.
17. Not to plead for him.
18. Not to refrain from testifying against him.
19. Not to prophesy in the name of idolatry.
20. Not to listen to such prophesy.
21. Not to prophesy falsely even in the name of the Lord.
22. Not to fear to destroy a false prophet.
23. Not to swear in the name of idolatry.
24. Not to practise necromancy.
25. Not to practise sorcery.
26. Not to sacrifice to Moloch (burning first born in sacrifice).
27. Not to set up a pillar.
28. Not to bow down to a figure made of stone.
29. Not to plant a grove.

30. To destroy idols and their belongings.
31. Not to benefit from idol worship and its belongings.
32. Not to enjoy their plated ornaments.
33. Not to make a covenant with idolaters.
34. Not to show them favours.
35. Not to let them dwell in our land.
36. Not to follow their customs or dress.
37. Not to practise witchcraft.
38. Not to practise divination.
39. Not to practise augury.
40. Not to practise enchantment.
41. Not to seek the spirits of the dead.
42. Not to consult those who practice spiritualism.
43. Not to consult augurers.
44. Not to practise magic.[1]
45. Not to round off the side curls of the head.
46. Not to destroy the corners of the beard.
47. Man shall not adorn himself in women's clothes.
48. A woman shall not adorn herself in armour or the clothes of a man.
49. Not to practise tattooing.
50. Not to lacerate oneself.
51. Not to tear one's hair for the dead.

An elucidation of all these commandments is given in the following chapters.

Chapter 1

1. In the days of Enosh[2] the children of mankind erred grievously and rejected the advice of the wise men of that generation, and Enosh himself suffered from that. Their mistake was to say that 'because God[3] made the stars and planets to rule the universe and placed them on high to share honour with them, for they are ministers who render service in His presence, they are worthy of praise, glory and honour'. They also said that, 'It is the will of God — blessed

1 See Deuteronomy 18:10.
2 The grandson of Adam (Genesis 4:26).
3 The word *El* is used here.

be He — to exalt and honour what He exalted and honoured, just as a king desires to honour those who stand before him: such is the prerogative of a king'. When this idea arose in their hearts, they began to build temples, to offer sacrifices, and to praise and glorify them in words. Because of a wrong belief they bowed down before the stars in order to reach the will of the Creator. This is the basis of idolatry and was the verbal tradition of the worshippers who knew its origin. They did not say that there was no god except one special star. Jeremiah said: 'Who would not fear Thee, O King of nations? for to Thee doth it appertain ... there is none like unto Thee. But they are altogether brutish and foolish; the stock is a doctrine of vanities' (Jeremiah 10:7-8), meaning 'All know that Thou art alone, but by mistakes and folly they think that vanity is Thy will'.

2.   After a long time there arose among the children of men false prophets who said that God had commanded them to serve such and such a star, or all the stars. They brought offerings and libations to drink in certain quantities, built a temple and made an image for all the people, men, women and children to bow down before it. A prophet made it known that an image, which he had invented in his heart, was the form of a particular star, revealed to him in prophecy. In this way, they began to make images in the temples and under groves, and on the hill tops and high places where they congregated and bowed down. The people were told that 'this image did good or evil and was worthy of worship and awe'. The priests said to them that by 'such service you will prosper and have good fortune, so do so and so, or don't do so and so'. Then other deceivers arose who said that the star itself, or the planet or messenger had spoken with them and told them to serve the idol and to worship it by doing one thing and not another. The service of images by different ceremonies with sacrifice and bowing down before them spread throughout the world. After a long time the great and awful Name was forgotten and the people, men, women and children, only recognised an image of wood or stone and the temple of stone which they had been brought up from infancy to serve by bowing down, and by swearing by its name. The wise men among them, the priests and such like, thought that there was no god except the stars and planets whose images were made in their likenesses. So the Rock of the universe had no one to recognise Him except solitary persons like Enosh, Methuselah, Noah, Shem and Eber. Thus

the world continued to revolve until a pillar of the world was born — Abraham, our father.

3.   When this mighty one grew up, he began to think hard. Even when young, he thought by day and night and wondered how it was possible for the universe to revolve without a driver to turn it, for it was impossible for it to do that by itself. He had no teacher or instruction in the matter, for he was sunk in Ur of the Chaldees among foolish idolaters. His father and mother and all the people worshipped the stars, and he worshipped with them. His heart struggled to reach the way of Truth and to understand the correct line of thought. He realised that there was one God who led the planets and that He had created all and that there was no other god except Him. He knew that all were mistaken and that what caused them to err was worship of the images which drove the Truth out of their minds. Abraham was forty years old when he recognised his Creator and, as soon as he recognised and understood, he began to think of changing the sons of Ur of the Chaldees to spread judgment among them and to teach that theirs was not the way of truth. He broke the images and began to tell the people that it was proper to worship only the Lord of the Universe, to bow down to Him and to offer sacrifice and drink offerings so that all future creatures might recognise Him. It was proper to destroy and smash the idols so that the people should not err by them like those who think there is no god save images. When he had won them by his evidence, the king sought to kill him and by a miracle he escaped to Haran. There he stood up and made known to all that there was one God in the Universe who should be served and whom he proclaimed. He went forward from city to city and from country to country until he reached the land of Canaan and proclaimed the Name of the Lord, as the verse states: 'Abraham called there on the name of the Lord, the everlasting God' (Genesis 21:33). When the people collected round him and questioned him about his words, he explained to each according to his intelligence until he turned them to the way of Truth. Thousands and tens of thousands gathered and became Abraham's household and he planted in their hearts this great principle. He wrote books and taught Isaac his son, and Isaac taught and advised and instructed his son, Jacob and made him a teacher. Jacob our father taught all his children and appointed Levi head of the school of learning — to teach the way of the Lord and to fulfil

Abraham's commands. Jacob commanded his children not to cease continual support for the Levites so that learning might not be forgotten. So the movement advanced in strength among the sons of Jacob and their associates so that a people arose who knew the Lord. When the children of Israel had spent a long time in Egypt they relapsed into idolatry from local customs. But the tribe of Levi remained faithful to the commandments of their fathers and were never idolaters. Soon the root which Abraham had planted would have been uprooted and the children of Jacob would have returned to the errors of the world but for the love of the Lord for us. To maintain the oath with Abraham He appointed Moses, our master, as lord of all the prophets and made him His messenger. When Moses our teacher prophesied, the Lord chose the people of Israel for His inheritance and crowned them with the commandments. He made known to them the way of His service and what would be the judgment against idolatry and all its erring followers.

Chapter 2

1. The fundamental imperative about idolatry was that worship was not to be paid to any created thing such as a messenger, a planet, a star, one of the four elements or to anything produced from them. This applied even if the worshipper knew that the 'Lord He is God'. If he served any of these things, as they were originally served by Enosh and his generation, that was idolatry. This is what the Torah warns against in the verse, 'And lest thou lift up thine eyes unto heaven, and when thou seest the sun, and the moon, and the stars, even all the host of heaven, shouldest be driven to worship them' (Deuteronomy 4:19), which is to say: 'You shall not let your heart's eye wander and think that these are guiding the universe, because they are sent by the Lord to all the world and exist for ever, and therefore it is right to bow down and worship and serve them'. About this, He cautioned 'that your heart be not deceived' (Deuteronomy 11:16), which means 'lest your heart's thought be deceived by serving created things as intermediaries between you and the Creator'.

2. Idolaters have compiled many books about their worship, the principle of that worship, its acts and laws. The

Holy One — blessed be He! — commanded us not to read any of these books and not to think about them or any detail of their teaching. Even to gaze at images made by idolaters is forbidden, as the verse states: 'Turn ye not unto idols' (Leviticus 19:4). On this matter a verse states: 'Lest you seek their gods asking how did they worship them?' Even if you do not worship idols yourself you may not ask how they are worshipped because that causes one to turn to idolaters and to do as they do, as has been said: 'Even so will I do'.

3.   All these prohibitions refer to one subject, the rejection of idolatry, and one who turns to and practices it deserves to be flogged. Thought has to be turned not only from idolatry but also from anything which might lead a man to root up a fundamental principle of the Torah. We are warned not to allow such thoughts to rise in our hearts, not to consider them in the mind, and not to think and be drawn to such imaginings of the heart, because man's understanding is limited and not all minds are able to reach perfect truth. If every man followed the imaginings of the heart, the world would be laid waste by the lack of understanding. For example, at some time a man would turn to idolatry, at other times to meditation upon the unity of the Creator who might or might not be; upon what is above or below or in front or behind, upon whether prophecy is true or not, and upon whether the Torah is from heaven or not. So not knowing the rules by which to judge that truth is perfect, he turns to heresy. In this matter the Torah gives warning for it states, 'that ye seek not after your own heart and your own eyes' (Numbers 15:39); this means 'do not let anyone be drawn by his limited understanding to think that his idea is the truth. The sages said that 'after one's own heart' meant atheism and 'after your own eyes' meant prostitution. Breaking the negative command, not to follow evil thought, may lead to banishment from the world to come, but is not punishable by lashes.

4.   The commandment about idolatry balances all other commands, as the verse states: 'And if ye have erred and not observed all these commandments, which the Lord hath spoken unto Moses' (Numbers 15:22). Tradition teaches that this referred to idolatry. Learn from this that whoever adopts idolatry denies all the Torah and all the prophets and all that the prophets had taught from the days of Adam to the end of the world as the verse states: 'from the day that the Lord commanded Moses, and henceforward among your genera-

tions' (Numbers 15:23). All who deny idolatry acknowledge the whole Torah, the prophets and what has been revealed to them since Adam to the end of the world. So this commandment becomes the most fundamental of all.

5. An Israelite who worshipped idols was like an idolater in every way, and not even like an Israelite who had committed a crime punishable by stoning. A convert to idolatry is an apostate from the whole Torah. The Israelite heretic was judged not to be an Israelite and was not accepted even as a penitent. The verse states: 'None that go unto her return again, neither take they hold of the paths of life' (Proverbs 2:19). Heretics were turned to the imagination of the heart by foolish talk, as we have mentioned, and they turned against the essence of Torah with insolence, contempt and a high hand, claiming that this was no iniquity. One is forbidden to talk with them or answer them in anything, as the verse states: 'come not nigh the door of her house' (Proverbs 5:8). The thought of a heretic is towards idolatry.

6. Anyone who accepts idolatry as truth, although he has not served idols, is shaming and blaspheming the exalted and aweful Name. An idolater is the same as one who blasphemes the Most High, and as was said, 'the soul that doeth ought presumptuously whether he be born in the land or a stranger, the same reproacheth the Lord' (Numbers 15:30). Therefore an idolater and blasphemer were both stoned and their bodies hung up in public. This is why I have included the law of blasphemy in this section on idolatry, for both of them deny the foundation of the Torah.

7. These are the laws concerning a blasphemer. He was not punished by stoning unless he pronounced the particular Name of four letters — *Aleph, Daleth, Nun* and *Yod* — or cursed it in one of the names which may not be erased. The verse states: 'And he that blasphemeth the name of the Lord, he shall surely be put to death and all the congregation shall certainly stone him' (Leviticus 24:16). If he used the particular Name he was punishable by stoning; by using other names he was punishable by warning and stripes. There are some who maintain that stoning was applied only when the Name [1] was used but I am of the opinion that the user of both particular names *Adonai* and *Jehovah* was stoned.

8. Where is the warning about blasphemy? The verse states: 'Thou shalt not revile the gods nor curse the ruler of thy people' (Exodus 22:28). In a trial for blasphemy wit-

[1] See Treatise 1, Chapter 6.

nesses were examined every day about the name used, and in giving evidence used substitute names of four letters instead of uttering the peculiar Name. When an examination ended, the public were ordered out of the court and the main witness was asked to repeat exactly what he heard. When he had spoken, the judges stood and rent their garments — and these were never mended. The second witness stated 'I also heard as he has said'; and if there were many witnesses, each one answered 'I also heard it'.

9.   If a blasphemer withdrew as soon as he had uttered the curse, this was worthless since he had blasphemed in the presence of witnesses and he deserved to be stoned. One who blasphemed the Holy Name in the name of an idol might be harmed by zealous people and destroyed. If the zealots did not destroy him, he was brought to the *Beth Din.* He was not stoned unless he had cursed using the peculiar Name of the Holy One.

10.   If one heard the Holy name being blasphemed, even if the blasphemer used a synonym, provided the blasphemer was an Israelite, he was obliged to rend his garment. Whether he heard the blasphemy directly or from a witness, it was rent. But if he heard it from an idolater, the garment was not rent. Eliakim and Shebna rent their garments only because Rabshakeh was an apostate Israelite (2 Kings 18:13-19). At such trials all the witnesses and judges layed their hands one after another on the head of the blasphemer and said: 'Your blood be on your own head, you brought it on yourself'. Blasphemy was the only crime when the death sentence was accompanied by laying on of hands, for the verse says: 'let all that heard him lay their hands upon his head' (Leviticus 24:14).

Chapter 3

1.   Anyone who worshipped idols of his own free will and wantonly, deserved to be cut off,[1] and if there were witnesses and a warning[2] had been given, he was sentenced to be stoned. If he had worshipped by mistake, he had to bring the statutory sin-offering.

2.   Idolaters fixed many forms of worship for each idol or figure which differed from one another. For example, a *peor*

[1] Probably meaning excommunicated by the community, and life shortened by God.

[2] Witnesses and a given warning were demanded in capital cases.

required a man to expose himself before it and a *merkolis*[1] was worshipped by casting stones at it or in front of it, and many other ways were ordained for other idols. Thus, if one exposed onself to a *merkolis* or threw stones at a *peor,* one was not culpable unless one worshipped in the proper way; as the verse states: 'How did these nations serve their gods? even so will I do likewise' (Deuteronomy 12:30). Hence it was necessary for the *Beth Din* to know the methods of worship in idolatry, for no one might be stoned unless the mode of worship was clear.

3.   The prohibition about these forms of worship and such like is written: 'ye shall not serve them' (Exodus 20:5 and Deuteronomy 5:9). To what do these words apply? To all the above services. Also anyone who worshipped an idol by bowing down, sacrifices, incense burning and libations was guilty, although it was not the idol's specific mode of worship. For example, if he offered a libation to a *poer* or sacrifices to a *merkolis,* he was guilty, as the verse says: 'He that sacrificeth unto any god, save unto the Lord only, he shall be utterly destroyed' (Exodus 22:20). Sacrifice was a general form of worship, so why was one told that a special kind of service was to be given to the Holy Name and that to offer it to another god was an offence worthy of stoning, whether the mode was correct or not? And similarly, all service peculiar to the Holy Name if given to another, whether in the correct mode or not, was an offence. The verse says about this: 'For thou shalt worship no other god' (Exodus 34:14). There was guilt in bowing down, even if it was not the appropriate form of worship for that idol and also in incense burning and libations. So stone throwing and libations were one and the same thing.

4.   One who spread excrement on an idol or offered a vessel of urine as a libation was guilty. If he killed a locust for it, that was excused unless such was the proper way of serving that idol. Also, if one slaughtered a deformed animal, one was free unless such was the correct mode of worship. If an idol was worshipped with a rod and he broke the rod, he was guilty and the wood could no longer be used. If he threw a stick in front of it, he was guilty and the stick could not be used. Throwing a stick was not like sprinkling blood; the stick remained whole while the blood was scattered. Anyone who accepted any kind of idol as a god deserved stoning,

[1] A pillar surmounted by a head of Mercury, who in this guise was the patron deity of wayfarers.

even if he took a brick and said 'thou art my god'. Such talk
was punishable and even if he recanted at once and said 'this
is not my god', repentance was not valid and he was stoned.
5.   The worshipper of an idol was guilty, even if he did it
in a manner which disgraced that idol. For example, if one
exposed onself to a *peor* in order to be contemptuous or
threw a stick at a *merkolis* in contempt, he was guilty
because such was an accepted mode of worship. If he did it
by mistake, he was obliged to bring a sin-offering.
6.   He who worshipped idols out of love, as when he
delighted in an image for its fine workmanship, or because
he feared it might harm him — as they do who imagine that
such worship brings good or evil — and if such a person took
that idol as a god, he deserved to be stoned; but unless he
served it in its proper manner or in one of the four ways,[1] he
was not culpable. He who embraced an idol with kisses, or
prostrated himself before it, or who washed and anointed it,
or put shoes and garments on it to honour it, violated the
negative commandment which states: 'Thou shalt not bow
down to their gods, nor serve them' (Exodus 23:24) and such
attentions to the idol are included in service. However, lashes
were not inflicted upon him for doing any of these, as none
of them was specifically mentioned in detail. If one's attention was the accepted mode of serving that idol and he
intended to worship it, he was guilty.
7.   If a thorn got into a man's foot when he was near an
idol, he might not stoop to take it out lest he might have
appeared to be bowing down. If some of his money was
scattered before it, he might not bend to collect it lest he
appeared to bow down, but he might sit down and collect it.
8.   One had to be careful when drinking water that his
mouth should not touch the face of an ornamental fountain,
lest he might appear to have been kissing it.
9.   Anyone who made an idol, although he did not make it
for himself or worship it, was striped. The verse says: 'Thou
shalt not make unto thee any graven image, or any likeness'
(Exodus 20:4 and Deuteronomy 5:8). Also, whoever made
an idol with his own hand for others, even for an idolater,
was lashed. The verse says: 'nor make to yourselves molten
gods' (Leviticus 19:4). He who made an idol for himself was
lashed twice.
10.   It was forbidden to make images for beauty's sake, even
if not for idolatry. The verse says: 'Ye shall not make with

[1] See paragraph 3.

me gods of silver' (Exodus 20:23), which means that figures made of silver and gold, although merely beautiful, may cause people to think that they are for idolatry. This prohibition applied to human forms only. A human shape in wood or clay or stone might not be made. If the shape was made in relief, for example on a stone figure or vessel in a palace, the maker was lashed, but if the figure was merely drawn or was a sign like those on boards or tablets, or was woven on a rug, it was permissible.

11. A ring on which a human form was engraved in relief was not to be cherished but might be used to stamp a seal. If the form was only engraved, it might be worn but it might not be used as a seal because the stamp would make a form in relief. It was forbidden to make an image of the sun, the moon, the stars and planets, and the ministering servants. The verse says: 'You shall not make for Me', meaning any likeness of My messengers who minister to Me on high, not even on a tablet. Forms of animals and other living creatures — excluding man — and of trees, plants and such like were allowed even if made in relief.

Chapter 4

1. Those who led a city of Israel astray, even when they themselves were not idolaters, were stoned, if they seduced the inhabitants of their city to serve idols. The citizens of the corrupted city were slain by the sword if they had served idols or accepted an idol as their god. Where is the warning against leading astray? The verse says: 'Neither let it be heard out of thy mouth' (Exodus 23:13).

2. No city was pronounced seduced unless the seducers belonged to it and were of the same tribe. The verse says: 'Certain men, the children of Belial, are gone out from among you, and have withdrawn the inhabitants of their city, saying, Let us go and serve other gods, which ye have not known' (Deuteronomy 13:13). The seducers had to be two or more men for the verse said: 'men, children of Belial' and in number the seduced had to be at least a hundred or the majority of a tribe. When the majority of a tribe were seduced, they were judged individually. If the verse says the inhabitants of a city, it means neither a small hamlet nor a large district. A small hamlet contained less than a hundred people and the majority of a tribe meant a large district. If the seducers were women or children or a single person or

only a few went astray, or were corrupted by an outsider, they were judged individually for idolatry and the guilty were stoned. Their belongings were dealt with, as was customary, when the *Beth Din* pronounced a death sentence.

3.   A city might be pronounced seduced by a *Beth Din* of seventy-one members,[1] as the verse states: 'Then shalt thou bring forth that man or that woman, which have committed that wicked thing, unto thy gates' (Deuteronomy 17:5). Thus individuals were condemned to death by the courts at each gate but many were not sentenced to death save by the great *Beth Din*.

4.   No city of refuge could be named as a seduced city, since the verse states: 'within any of thy gates' (Deuteronomy 17:2); nor might Jerusalem be pronounced a seduced city because it was not divided among the tribes. Also a frontier city might not be pronounced seduced lest idolaters should collect in it and destroy the Land of Israel. One court could not judge three cities if they were adjacent, but it could if they were far apart.

5.   No city could be judged to be seduced unless the seducers had spoken in the plural, saying 'let us go and worship' or 'let us go and sacrifice' or 'let us burn incense' or 'let us offer libations' or 'let us go and bow down and accept it as a god' and they heard it and worshipped it in the correct way, or in one of the four forms of worship. If in a seduced city all these conditions were not fulfilled, what was done with it? Each individual who had served idols was warned and, if he persisted, he was stoned and his property passed to his heirs.

6.   How was a seduced city judged? When it was apparent that it was truly seduced and the great *Beth Din* had sent representatives to inquire and investigate, and it was clear that the whole city or the majority of the people had turned to idolatry. After that, two learned envoys were sent to warn the people to repent. If they repented, it was well. If they stood by their evil, the *Beth Din* commanded all Israel to rise against them in force and to make war against them until the city was captured. Then the *Beth Din* judged them. If two witnesses testified that a person had been warned and yet continued to serve idols, he was separated. If only a minority were idolaters, they were stoned and the rest of the city was spared. If the majority worshipped idols, they were taken to

[1] A great *Beth Din (Sanhedrin)* of seventy-one members (Numbers 11:16).

the great *Beth Din* and tried, and all the guilty were slain by the sword. If the whole city was seduced, every man and their women and children were put to the sword. If the majority served idols, only the families of those were slain by the sword. The seducers were stoned whether the entire city or a majority had been seduced. All booty was collected in the main street, as the verse states: 'And thou shalt gather all the spoil of it into the midst of the street and shalt burn with fire the city and all the spoil thereof' (Deuteronomy 13:16). The living animals were killed and all booty was burned. The burning was mandatory. If there was no main street, the spoil was placed outside the city and enclosed by a wall continuous with the city boundary.

7.   The property of the righteous among them — the remnant of the inhabitants who were not seduced with the majority — was burned with the rest of the booty. It was destroyed because they had continued to live there. Anyone who benefited from any of these goods was lashed once. The verse says: 'And there shall cleave nought of the cursed thing to thine hand' (Deuteronomy 13:17).

8.   If witnesses of a seduced city were found to be false, their property could be taken over by anyone because the witnesses were declared to be false. How was this allowed? Because such witnesses lost their property as soon as such a sentence was pronounced. A seduced city was never rebuilt and anyone doing so was lashed. The verse says: 'It shall not be built again' (Deuteronomy 13:16). It could be used for gardens and orchards. The saying 'it shall not be built again' meant not built again as a place of habitation as it had been before.

9.   Caravans passing from one place to another, which came into a seduced city and were corrupted and stayed there thirty days, were slain by the sword and their property was destroyed. If they stayed less than thirty days, they were stoned and their property was given to their heirs.

10.   The property of a man of another district stored in a seduced city was not burned although the inhabitants had accepted liability for it. It was returned to its owners, for the verse states: 'the spoil of it', not spoil of neighbours. If the property of seduced evil-doers deposited in another district could be collected, it was burned with all the rest, but if it could not be, it was given to the heirs.

11.   As regards domestic animals in the seduced city which were shared with another city, they were forbidden to be

eaten, but dough might be used because it could be divided.

12. An animal of a seduced city which had been ritually slaughtered was forbidden — like an ox sentenced to stoning [1] and already killed. Hair of the head, whether of men or women [2], might be kept but locks cut off as booty were forbidden.

13. Fruits on the trees were allowed, for the verse says: 'And thou shalt collect all the spoil of it into the midst of the street thereof and shalt burn with fire the city' (Deuteronomy 13:16), that is, such spoils as were collected were burned but fruits which needed to be picked were exempt. Needless to say, the trees themselves were allowed and, of course, belonged to the heirs. Dedicated things such as animals for the altar for sacrifice were killed, for 'The sacrifice of the wicked is abomination' (Proverbs 21:27). The holy things for the upkeep of the Temple were ransomed and buried. The verse says 'spoil of it' but not spoil of Heaven (Deuteronomy 13:16).

14. The firstborn, the tithes which were in the city, the unblemished animals dedicated for sacrifice were killed, and the deformed among them were destroyed with the other things. The heave-offerings were left to rot if they had been already in the possession of a priest for they belonged to him, but if they were still in the hand of an Israelite they were given to a priest of another region because they were the property of Heaven and already sanctified.

15. Second tithes [3] and money for second tithes and sacred writings were hidden.

16. Whoever meted out judgment on a seduced city was surely as one who had brought a burnt offering. The verse states, 'every whit, for the Lord thy God' (Deuteronomy 13:16). Also, he turned away the Lord's great anger from Israel. The verse states, 'that the Lord may turn from the fierceness of his anger, and shew thee mercy, and have compassion upon thee, and multiply thee' (Deuteronomy 13:17).

Chapter 5

1. The enticer of an individual Israelite, whether a man or woman, was stoned even if neither he nor the enticed had served idolatry, because he had taught the worship. It

[1] Exodus 21:28
[2] Wigs
[3] Deuteronomy 14:22f.

mattered not whether this seducer was a layman or a prophet, whether a single man or woman or several people; they died by stoning.

2.   The tempter of the majority of the people in a city was called a seducer, not an enticer. If such a tempter was a prophet, his punishment was stoning and the enticed were judged individually, not like the inhabitants of a seduced city, unless there were two enticers. If an enticer said 'the idol told me to serve it' or 'the Holy One told me to worship idols', it was the same as if he were a corrupting prophet and, if he tempted most of the city, he was stoned. The enticer was stoned whether he spoke in the singular or plural. For example, if one said to a friend 'I am going to worship idols', 'I am going, let us go and worship in the way arranged for that idol', 'I will sacrifice, let us go and sacrifice', 'I will burn incense, let us go and do so', 'I will offer a libation, let us go and give a drink offering', 'I will bow down, let us go and bow down', that was enticing. If two were enticed, then there were two witnesses to bring him before the *Beth Din* and to give evidence that he had spoken thus to them, and they would stone him.

3.   An enticer need not be given a warning.[1]   If he has spoken to only one person, that person should say, 'I have a friend who wants to hear about this'. Then the enticer exposes himself before two witnesses and so may be sentenced to death. Of the capital offences enumerated in the Torah, this is the only one in which spying is allowed. For example, a spy brought two witnesses to a place and hid them in the dark where they could see the enticer and hear his words, but he could not see them. The spy then asked the tempter to repeat what he had said to him when they were alone. If the tempter did so, the spy answered, 'How can we deny our Lord in the Heavens and go and serve bits of wood and stone?' If the enticer repented or was silent, he was guiltless, but if he answered 'It is mandatory and right to do it', the two witnesses stood up and took him to the *Beth Din* and the sentence was stoning.

4.   It is a positive command that the hand of the spy shall slay him, as the verse says: 'thine hand shall be first upon him to put him to death' (Deuteronomy 13:9). The enticed might not make friends with the enticer. The verse says: 'Thou shalt not consent unto him nor hearken unto him' (Deuteronomy

[1] In capital cases in Israel, judgment required two witnesses and a given warning.

13:8). Yet do not think that because elsewhere it is said of an enemy 'thou shalt surely help him' (Exodus 23:5) that you can help an enticer. Further think not that because it is written, 'neither shalt thou stand against the blood of thy neighbour' (Leviticus 19:16), that it is impossible to stand against the blood of this one. Torah teaches, 'Neither shall thine eye pity him (Deuteronomy 13:8). The informer is also forbidden to speak of the tempter's deserts. The same verse continues 'neither shalt thou spare, neither shalt thou conceal him'. One who knew anything against a tempter was not allowed to remain silent. The warning to a layman who is an enticer is derived from the verse, 'And all Israel shall hear, and fear' (Deuteronomy 13:11).

5.   One who enticed others to worship him by saying 'worship me', and they did so, was stoned. If they did not, he was not stoned even if they had listened to him attentively and said 'yes'. However, if the enticer had enticed them to worship another man or other kinds of idolatry, if they listened and said 'yes, let us go and worship' both enticer and enticed were stoned, even although the worship had not been performed, even as the verse states: 'Thou shalt not consent unto him, nor hearken unto him' (Deuteronomy 13:8). Therefore, if one listened and consented, one was guilty.

6.   What of a prophet who prophesied in the name of idolatry? For example, someone might say, 'I was told by some idol or a star commanded me to do so and so or not to do it'; although his intent may have been to keep the Law, to condemn the unclean and to purify the pure, if he had been warned before two witnesses, he was hanged. The verse states: 'The prophet that shall speak in the name of other gods, even that prophet shall die' (Deuteronomy 18:20). The general warning about this is, 'make no mention of the name of other gods' (Exodus 23:13).

7.   It was forbidden to argue with and answer anyone who prophesied in the name of idolatry or to ask him for a sign[1] or miracle. If he gave one, no attention or thought was given to it; anyone who meditated upon the truth of his signs violated a negative command; 'Thou shalt not hearken unto the words of that prophet' (Deuteronomy 13:3). Likewise, a false prophet was hanged, although he spoke in the name of the Lord and did not add or take away anything of the Torah. The verse says: 'But the prophet, which shall presume

[1] To give a sign meant usually to quote a verse of the Torah to confirm your statement.

to speak a word in My name, which I have not commanded him to speak, or that shall speak in the name of other gods, even that prophet shall die' (Deuteronomy 18:20).

8.   If a prophet prophesied what he had not heard in a prophetic vision, or if he used words of another fellow and claimed that they had been spoken to him in a vision, he was a false prophet and the punishment was hanging.

9.   Anyone who withholds himself from pronouncing a death sentence against a false prophet because of his eminence in the path of prophecy violated the negative command which says; 'Thou shalt not be afraid of him' (Deuteronomy 18:22). Likewise, anyone withholding himself from testifying against him or fearing him and dreading his words was included amongst those who violate the commandments. A false prophet was judged only by a *Beth Din* of seventy-one members (Sanhedrin).

10.   Anyone making a vow in the name of an idol or swearing by it was lashed. The verse states: 'and make no mention of the name of other gods' (Exodus 23:13). It was the same whether the vow was for himself or the idol. It was forbidden to swear to an idolater by what he feared or even to mention the name of his idol incorrectly — the verse says, 'make no mention'.

11.   A man might not say to another 'wait for me beside such and such an idol' or use similar expressions. All idols written about in Holy Writ were allowed to be named, for example, *peor, baal, nebo, gaad* and the like. It was forbidden to cause others to vow or take oaths in the name of idolatry, but a person was only punished by lashes when he swore by the name of the idol to support himself by swearing.

Chapter 6

1.   He who practised necromancy or spiritualism of his free will and wantonly deserved to be excommunicated and, if due warning had been given and there were two witnesses, he deserved to be stoned. If he acted by mistake, he had to bring a sin offering. How was necromancy practised? Someone stood and burned special incense waving a twig of myrtle in his hand and murmuring words known to necromancers which the listener heard as a low voice speaking to him from the depth of the earth and scarcely audible but as if it was

felt by the mind[1]: or someone held a skull with incense burning in it and a low voice came out of the skull and answered questions. All such were practising necromancy and those who performed it were worthy of stoning.

2. How was spiritualism practised? Someone placed a special bird's bone in his mouth, burned incense and did other things until he fell in a fit like an epileptic and uttered words about the future. A warning against all these types of idolatry is in the verse: 'Regard not them that have familiar spirits, neither seek after wizards' (Leviticus 19:31).

3. Any man who gave up his children to Moloch, willingly and wantonly, deserved to be excommunicated. If he did it by mistake, he brought a sin offering. If he did it before witnesses and a warning had been given, he was stoned. The verse states: 'Whosoever ... giveth any of his seed unto Molech, he shall surely be put to death' (Leviticus 20:2). Where is the prohibition? The verse states: 'And thou shalt not let any of thy seed pass through the fire to Moloch' (Leviticus 18:21), and further: 'There shall not be found among you anyone that maketh his son or his daughter to pass through the fire' (Deuteronomy 18:10). How was this performed? A great fire was lit and a man took some of his children and handed them over to the priests who served the idol. The priests gave the boys and girls back after passing them through the fire with the father's permission, or the father, with permission of the priests, passed his son through the flames on his feet from one side of the fire to the other. The child was not to be burned, as was done to sons and daughters of other idol worshippers, and 'passing through the flames' was itself service to the name of Moloch. Anyone doing this in the service of other idols was not serving Moloch.

4. A man was not deemed deserving of excommunication or stoning unless he handed over his son to Moloch and caused him to walk on foot through the fire in the correct way. If he handed him over but did not lead him, or if he led him but did not hand him over, or if he handed him over and passed him in the wrong way, he was not guilty. Neither was he guilty until he had handed over only some of his children and left others, since the verse says: 'Whosoever ... giveth any one of his seed to Moloch', that is some but not all.[2]

[1] Ventriloquy.

[2] Various excuses to avoid a capital sentence, because duress was so often used in such situations.

5.   Whether the children were legitimate or illegitimate, they were his own sons, and daughters or grandchildren and he was guilty because they were the seed of his loins. But if he led a brother or sister or his parents or was himself led through, he was not guilty. If he led through a child who was asleep or blind, he was not guilty.[1]

6.   The kind of pillar which the Torah forbad was a building where the people collected in the Lord's name and even worshipped but this was an idolatrous custom, as the verse states: 'Neither shalt thou set thee up any image' (Deuteronomy 16:22). Whoever set up such a pillar was lashed. With regard to the flat stone mentioned in the Torah, if one bowed down on it in the name of the Holy One, one was lashed because it was said: 'Neither shall ye set up any image of stone in your land, to bow down unto it' (Leviticus 26:1). It was an idolatrous custom to lay a stone before the idol and bow down upon it. The Lord was not to be worshipped thus. A man was not lashed unless he spread his hands and feet on such a stone, lying upon it. That was the 'bowing down' which was spoken of in the Torah.

7.   Where did these rules apply? In any place except the Temple where one was allowed to bow down on the stones. The verse states: 'in your land' (Leviticus 26:1), meaning in your own land you may not bow down on stones but only on the paved stones in the Temple.[2] Because of this all Israelites used to spread out coverings or put straw and chaff on the paved synagogue floors to separate them from the stones. If no substance could be found to separate one from the stone, one went to another place to bow down or bent sideways, turning so that the face might not touch the stone.

8.   Anyone who bowed down to the Lord on cut stones and did not spread hands and feet was not lashed, but was given a rebel's beating. As regards idolatry, whether the hands and feet were spread or not, if his face touched the ground, he deserved stoning.

9.   Whoever planted a tree near the altar or Temple court, whether a barren or fruit tree, and whether he did it to beautify or adorn the Temple, was striped. The verse states: 'Thou shalt not plant thee a grove of any trees near unto the altar of the Lord thy God' (Deuteronomy 16:21). It was the

[1] Various excuses to avoid a capital sentence, because duress was so often used in such situations.

[2] Only once a year on the Day of Atonement does the congregation in Israel kneel down.

custom of idolaters to plant trees at the side of an altar and to collect the people there.

10. It was forbidden to make a wooden entrance to the Temple, like those in courtyards near the altar, even though the wood was built in and not part of a tree planted near the altar, since the verse says 'any kind of wood'. The corridors and also cornices projecting from the Temple walls were of stone, not of wood.

Chapter 7

1. It was a positive commandment to destroy idolatry and its services and everything made for it, as the verse states: 'Ye shall utterly destroy all the places' (Deuteronomy 12:2), and: 'But thus shall ye deal with them' (Deuteronomy 7:5). Within the Land of Israel it was mandatory to uncover idolatry and to destroy it in 'Our Land'. Outside Israel the people were not commanded to pursue idolaters, but when they had conquered a district they destroyed the idolatry therein, the verse states: 'Ye shall ... destroy the names of them out of that place' (Deuteronomy 12:3). Idolatry within Israel was to be uncovered but not outside it.

2. Idolatry, its articles of worship and what was offered to and made for idols were all forbidden as sources of benefit, as the verse states: 'Neither shalt thou bring an abomination into thine house' (Deuteronomy 7:26). Anyone benefiting in any way was striped twice; once because the verse says 'neither shalt thou bring', and once more because it says, 'And there shall cleave nought of the cursed thing to thine hand' (Deuteronomy 13:17).

3. If an animal was offered to an idol completely, it was forbidden to profit from it even from its manure, bones, horns, hoof or hide: from all these no benefit was allowed. Thus if there was a mark on a hide indicating that it was from an animal sacrificed to idolatry, such as a tear over the area of the heart,[1] the hide was forbidden as a source of benefit, and this applied in similar circumstances.

4. What was the difference between the idol of an idolater and one which belonged to an Israelite? The idol of an idolater was absolutely forbidden as beneficial property. The verse says: 'The graven images of their gods shall ye burn with fire' (Deuteronomy 7:25), meaning as soon as it becomes a god to the idolater. That of an Israelite was not

---

[1] One of the negative commands was not to use or take out part of a living animal.

forbidden until it had been worshipped, as the verse says: 'Putteth it in a secret place' (Deuteronomy 27:15); things done in secret implied worship. Things used in the service of idolaters whether by an idolater or an Israelite, were not forbidden until they had been used to serve idols.

5. Anyone who made an idol for another, although he was striped, was allowed to keep the wages even if it was made for an idolater, because the idol did not become forbidden until it was completed and the last stroke that completed it was not even worth a penny to him. Anyone taking scrap material from an idolater and finding idols in it, if he had paid but not yet taken possession, might return them to the idolater. Likewise, if he had taken possession without payment, he returned it, even if taking possession was considered by the idolater to complete the deal. That constituted 'purchase in error'. If he had both paid and carried it away, he had to throw the thing into the Dead Sea![1]   When an idolater and a proselyte each inherited from an idolatrous father, the proselyte could say to the idolater: 'You take the idol and I the money', 'You take the libation to be used for the idol and I the fruit'. But if the idol had fallen into the proselyte's possession, this was not permitted.

6. Images made by idolaters for their beauty could be enjoyed but images made for idolatry were forbidden. How could they be identified? All images found in villages were forbidden because it was assumed that they were made for idolatry. Of images found in cities, if they were placed at the city gates and held in their hands a staff, a bird, a ball, a sword, a crown or a ring, then it was assumed that they were idols and so forbidden. If not, they were judged for their beauty and permitted.

7. Discarded images of idol worship found in the market or among junk were permitted and, needless to say, broken images, except that the hand of an image of a star or planet, or a foot or limb were forbidden property, because there was no doubt that such was part of an idol that had been worshipped. Hence it was forbidden until it was known that the idolaters had considered it to be useless.

8. If one found vessels or vestments on which there were golden or silver images of the sun and moon or of a serpent, and if such were engraved on nose-rings or other rings all these were forbidden. But if images were engraved on other

---

[1] Meaning get rid of completely.

utensils, it was assumed that they were for beauty only, and they were permitted.

9. Idolatry, its belongings and things offered to it were forbidden whatever they were, and idols mixed with beautiful structures even in one part in thousands were thrown into the Dead Sea. Similarly if a cup used in idolatry was mixed with many cups or a bit of meat mixed with other meat, all were thrown into the Dead Sea. Also if a hide with a heart-cut was mixed with other skins, no benefit might be had from any of them. If one erred and sold something idolatrous, or an idol's belongings, or offerings made to it, the price was confiscated. Everything belonging to idolatry was forbidden. The verse says: 'Neither shalt thou bring an abomination into thine house, lest thou be a cursed thing like it' (Deuteronomy 7:26), and this applied to everything pertaining to idols or offered in their service.

10. The ashes of an idol or an *asherah* (see glossary) might not be used for benefit nor the glowing embers of an idol, but the flame might be used for it has no substance. A doubtful thing relating to idolatry was forbidden but if doubly doubtful it was allowed. For example, if an idol's cup fell into a basket of cups, all were forbidden because everything connected with idols was. If one cup in such a collection was separated and fell among other cups, all were permitted to be used. If an idolatrous ring was mixed with many others and two of them fell into the sea, all those remaining were allowed because it could be said that the idolatrous ring was one of the two. If it was mixed with a hundred rings and these were divided, forty in one place and sixty in another, and the forty fell among other rings, they were all allowed; for it could be said that the forbidden ring was in the majority. But if the sixty fell among others, all were forbidden property.

11. It was forbidden to sit in the shade of the stem of an *asherah*, whether it was worshipped itself or an idol under it was worshipped; but one might pass under its branches and leaves. If this could be avoided by going any other way, it was forbidden to pass that way, but if there was no other way, one ran under it.

12. Young birds in a nest in the *asherah* which did not need the mother bird might be taken, but fledglings and eggs which depended on the mother bird were forbidden property since truly the *asherah* was essential for them. A nest on top

of the *asherah* was permitted to be used because the bird had brought the straws from another place.

13. Wood taken from an *asherah* was forbidden and, if it was used to heat an oven, the oven had to be cooled off and other wood used to relight it before baking in it. If one made bread in the oven without first cooling it, the bread could not be used. If such bread got mixed with other bread, the price of it was thrown into the Dead Sea, so as not to be of any benefit, and the other loaves were permitted property.

14. If one made a shuttle of wood from an *asherah* and wove a garment, the garment was forbidden. If the garment was mixed with other garments, its value might be cast into the Dead Sea, and then all the rest of the garments were allowed. One was allowed to plant vegetables in the shade of an *asherah*, both in summer when shade was needed and in the rainy season, because for growth the vegetables needed both the shade of the *asherah* which was forbidden and the soil which was not. Thus, when an action depended on both a forbidden and a permitted thing, permission was allowed; so a field which was manured with manure associated with idolatry might be seeded, and a cow fattened upon fodder associated with idolatry might be eaten, and so on.

15. Meat, wine or fruit collected for idol worship and brought to the idol's temple were not forbidden unless they had been laid before the idol. To bring them before the idol was sacrifice and, even if they were withdrawn later, they were still forbidden. The Torah forbade as a source of benefit anything found in an idol's temple, even water and salt, and anyone who ate a particle thereof was lashed.

16. If one found clothes or vessels or coins on an idol's head placed in a shameful manner, they could be used, but if they were placed respectfully, they were forbidden property. For example, if one found a bag tied round the idol's neck or a folded cloth on its head or a vessel upside down on its head, that was permitted property because it was placed in contempt. However, if anything was found the like of which was used as a sacrifice on an altar of the temple, it was forbidden. How did this apply? Things were permitted when found outside the place of worship, but if within, whether in honour or shame, whether correct for that altar or not, they were forbidden, even water and salt. As regards a *peor* or a *merkolis*, everything connected with them within or outside was forbidden. A *merkolis'* stones, or stones which appeared to belong to him, were forbidden.

17. When an idol's sanctuary contained a bath house or pleasure park, that might be enjoyed if no benefit was given to idolatry. If it was shared with others for profit, such as priests' dues, it might be enjoyed so long as no payment was made.

18. If there was an image in a bath house, one might bathe there if it was placed only for its beauty, not if it was for worship, as the verse says: 'Neither shalt thou serve their gods' (Deuteronomy 7:16) implying that they were forbidden only when they were treated as gods, but not when they were treated contemptuously by standing at the pool and micturating before them.

19. If an idol's knife was used to slaughter an animal, the animal was permitted property because an injury had been done with the knife. If it was a dangerous animal, it was forbidden property because something beneficial had been done with an article belonging to idolatry. Likewise, it was forbidden to cut off flesh with it because that was beneficial, but if the cutting had caused loss or destruction, that was allowed.[1]

Chapter 8

1. One was allowed to benefit from anything that the hand of man could not grasp or make, although it was worshipped. Therefore, mountains and hills worshipped by idolaters, trees planted originally for their fruits, public springs of water and domestic animals – all these might be enjoyed as well as fruit worshipped where it had grown up, and likewise cattle. Needless to say, animals assigned to idolatry were allowed to be eaten whether assigned for worship or sacrifice. How was this allowed? Prior to any act done to it in the name of idolatry. But if anything had been done, it became prohibited property, for example, if a blood vessel had been opened in the idol's name or if one had bartered or doubly bartered it in the name of idolatry. This applied if the animal was one's own. If one killed a neighbour's animal for idolatry or exchanged it, there was no prohibition for no one could make property forbidden which was not his own. Bowing down to virgin land did not make it forbidden property but

1 The principle was that if an idol's knife improved something, then that thing was forbidden, but if the thing was spoiled, then it was allowed.

93

if one dug wells, pits or caves for idolatrous practices, that made it forbidden.

2. To bow down to water escaping in a stream was forbidden, and to take the water up in the hand and worship it was also prohibited. Stones from a mountain which had loosened and had been worshipped as they lay were permitted property because man's hand had not held them.

3. If an Israelite placed a brick in a place for worship but did not bow down to it and an idolater came along and did so, then it was forbidden property because setting it up was a deliberate act. Likewise, if he stuck up an egg[1] and an idolater came and bowed down to it, it was forbidden. If he cut up a gourd and bowed down to it, that was forbidden. If he bowed down to half a gourd which was still attached to the other half, that was forbidden as they might share in worship . A tree originally planted for worship was forbidden property because it was the *asherah* spoken of in the Torah. If a tree had been planted and cut down and the branches dedicated in the name of an idol and then the stump was grafted or budded, and branched fresh branches, they if cut off, were forbidden, but the rest of the tree was allowed. Similarly, when a tree had been worshipped, although the trunk was allowed, all the branches, twigs and fruits were forbidden so long as it was worshipped. A tree whose fruits were guarded by idolaters who said that they intended to make a drink from it — to drink on the idol's feast day — was a forbidden tree because clearly it was an *asherah*. It was a custom to use the fruit of an *asherah* thus.

4. A tree under which an idol was set up was forbidden property so long as the idol remained. If the idol was taken away, the tree was permitted property because the tree itself had not been worshipped. A building originally erected by idolaters to be worshipped or a building which became worshipped for its beauty was forbidden. If a building was plastered and decorated anew in the name of an idol, all the added material, if removed, was forbidden because it had been made for worship, but the rest of the building was permitted property. If an idol was brought into a house one was forbidden to benefit from the house so long as the idol was there. When the idol was taken away, the house was allowed. A stone which was hewn originally for worship was forbidden; likewise a stone hewn and plastered and painted

[1] Meaning obscure; possibly an egg and halves of a gourd were fertility symbols.

and engraved for worship, even if it was a bare stone decorated for worship, was forbidden. If the material was removed, that was forbidden because it had been used for worship, but the remaining stone was allowed.

5.   The stone on which an idol was placed was forbidden so long as the idol remained upon it. If the stone was removed from underneath the idol, it was then permitted. If a man's house, which was near an idol's house, fell down, he was forbidden to rebuild it. What could he do? He withdrew his wall some distance and filled the space with thorns or filth so that the idol's house could not be extended. If his house and that of the idol were shared, his half was allowed and the idol's half forbidden including the stones, wood and sand.

6.   How was an idol destroyed and all its forbidden belongings and sacrifices? They were broken up and scattered in the wind or burned and the ashes cast into the Dead Sea.

7.   Although benefit was allowed from anything which a man's hand could not hold and which had been worshipped, such as a mountain, an animal or a tree, it was not allowed from any overlaid decoration, and anyone who did benefit from such was striped, as the verse states: 'Thou shalt not desire the silver or gold that is on them' (Deuteronomy 7.25).   Platings which covered idols were included among things used in their service.

8.   If an idolater abandoned his idol before it came into the hand of an Israelite, it was allowed. The verse says: 'The graven images of their gods shall ye burn with fire' (Deuteronomy 7:25). This was done if they fell into Israelite hands while still used as gods, but if they had been abandoned, they were allowed.

9.   The idol of an Israelite could never be abandoned even if it was shared with an idolater. Rejection of it was useless; it remained forbidden for ever and had to be hidden. Similarly, if an idolater's idol came into the hand of an Israelite, it could never be allowed even if the idolater rejected it later — it was forbidden property for ever. An Israelite could not reject idols even with the permission of an idolater. An infant or an insane idolater could not reject idols. If an idolater rejected an idol, whether it was his own or the property of another idolater, and even if an Israelite had forced him to do so, the rejection was valid. No one but an idolater could reject an idol. If the idol was rejected, so were all its belongings. If the belongings had been rejected,

the idol was prohibited until rejected. Anything sacrificed to an idol could not be repudiated.

10. How was an idol rejected? They cut off the tip of its nose, the tip of its ears, the tip of a finger, or smashed its face without taking any part away, or sold it to an Israelite goldsmith, and so rejected it completely. But if they pawned it or sold it to an idolater or to an Israelite who was not a goldsmith, if dirt fell on it and they did not clean it, if robbers stole it and they did not try to reclaim it, if they spat at it, passed urine on it, dragged it about, threw excrement at it, such acts were not rejection.

11. If an idol was abandoned when there was peace, it was allowed because it was obviously rejected. In wartime it was forbidden because war had prevented its use. The fragments of an idol which broke of itself were forbidden until the idol had been rejected. Therefore if fragments of an idol were found, they were forbidden because perhaps the idol had not been rejected. If among the pieces there were bits which could be repaired, every bit required rejection, but if they could not be joined together, as soon as one fragment was rejected all the pieces were.

12. The altar of an idol which had been damaged remained forbidden until most of it was pulled down by the idolater, but if the pedestal was damaged, it was allowed. What was a pedestal and what was an altar? The pedestal was one stone, an altar had many stones. How were the stone of a *merkolis* annulled? As soon as they were used for building or paving roads, and so on, they were allowed. How was an *asherah* rejected? The branches were torn off or saplings removed, a stick or rod made from it, or it was damaged unnecessarily; such acts rejected it. If it was pruned for its own good, it was forbidden property but the prunings were allowed. If it belonged to an Israelite, whether it was pruned for its own good or not, both it and the prunings were forbidden forever, for an idol owned by an Israelite might never be rejected.

Chapter 9

1. For three days before a festival of idolatry it was forbidden to buy from or sell durable goods to the idolaters, to loan to them or borrow from them, to receive or make payment on loans secured by note or pledge, but a verbal loan might be accepted because it was as if one had rescued some-

thing from them. Perishable goods, such as vegetables and cooked food, might be sold to idolaters, up to the feast day. Where did these rules apply? Only in the Land of Israel; in other lands, only on the festival day itself was one forbidden to do business with them. If on the three days mentioned above one traded with them, one was allowed to enjoy the proceeds. On the festival day itself no benefit might be derived.

2. One was not allowed to send a gift to a Samaritan on his birthday unless it was known that he did not contribute to idolatry and was not an idolater. Also, if a Samaritan sent a gift to an Israelite on a festival, it might not be accepted; but if the Israelite feared to make an enemy of him it might be accepted in his presence but not used until it was known that the Samaritan neither practised nor professed idolatry.

3. If the festival of a group of idol worshippers lasted for many days, they were all considered as one day and it and the three days preceeding the festival were forbidden.

4. The day when idolaters gathered to set up a king and they offered sacrifice and praise to their gods was treated like all their other festival days, but if an idolater made a feast to honour his star on his birthday, or made a festival on the day when he cut off his beard or plait, or when he returned from a voyage, or was released from prison, or for his son, on that day alone it was forbidden to deal with him. Likewise the day of a festival for the dead was a forbidden day and when goods and incense were burned after a death, it was certain that this was idolatry.

5. Festivals were only forbidden when an idol was served, but one was allowed to join with those who were just rejoicing and feasting and drinking as a common custom, or in honour to a king.

6. One was always forbidden to sell things to idolaters that were used specially in the service of the local idols; other goods were ordinary merchandise. If an idolater announced that he was making a purchase for idolatry, one was forbidden to sell it to him unless one damaged it to make it unfit to offer to that idol; faulty things might not be offered to idols.

7. If such special goods were mixed up with ordinary ones, for example, pure frankincense with black frankincense, they could be sold without fearing that the idolater would separate out the pure for worship.

8. Just as one was not allowed to sell to idolaters things

that would support idolatry, so one might not sell to them anything that was a public danger, for example, bears, lions, weapons, fetters and chains, nor might one sharpen their weapons. All things that one was forbidden to sell to an idolater one was forbidden to sell to an Israelite suspected of re-selling them to idolaters. It was also forbidden to sell weapons to Israelite robbers.

9.   Israelites, who lived among idolaters and with whom they were at peace were allowed to sell weapons to the king's servants and his army because they waged war against the enemies of the country and so they preserved peace and became a shield to our people dwelling among them.

10.   An idolatrous city was by-passed and not entered but if the idol worship went on outside the city, one might enter it. A traveller going from one place to another was not allowed to pass through an idolatrous city. How was this applied? When there was just one road to the place![1]   If there was another route, he ought to take that.

11.   It was forbidden to assist an idolater in building a shrine where an idol was to be set up. Yet if one transgressed and did it, his wages were allowed. He might, however, build a palace or courtyard around a shrine which was already there.

12.   In an idolatrous city where shops were decorated for idolatry or not decorated, the former were forbidden and their contents, because it was understood that such ornaments were for idolatry. Shops that were not ornamented might be used. It was forbidden to lease the shops of idolaters because that would benefit idolatry.

13.   If one sold a house to an idolater, the price was forbidden property and had to be cast into the Dead Sea. But if idolaters forced an Israelite, embezzled his house and stuck up an idol in it, the price was allowed and a complaint could be sent to their courts.[2]

14.   It was forbidden to play the funeral pipes of idolaters. One was allowed to go to an idolatrous fair to buy from them animals, servants and maidservants, houses and fields and vineyards, with written contracts lodged in their courts, because that was a means of escape from their power. How did this apply? When one had purchased from a private owner who did not pay taxes to idolatry; but purchase from merchants who paid taxes to idol worship and aided idolatry

1 One might be accused of going in to serve idols if the city had only one entrance.

2 A Jew normally tried to settle matters outside Gentile courts.

was forbidden. If one erred and dealt with a merchant and if the purchase was an animal, one cut the arteries below the knee; if it was material or utensils, they were left to rot; if one had taken money or metal goods, they were cast into the Dead Sea. If a servant had been bought, nothing could be done to him.

15. If an idolater made a feast for a son or daughter, one was forbidden to take part in the feast and even to partake of one's own food and drink there, since an Israelite was not allowed to sit in an idolater's company. How long was one forbidden to eat there? From the time when they began to prepare for the feast, all the days of the feast and for thirty days after it. If an idolater made a marriage festival, one was forbidden to eat with him, not only for thirty days but for twelve months after it. All these prohibitions separated one from idolatry, as the verse says: 'Lest one call thee, and thou eat of his sacrifice; and thou take of their daughters unto thy sons, and their daughters go a whoring after their gods' (Exodus 34:15-16).

16. A daughter of Israel might not suckle the child of an idolater because that would rear a child for idolatry. Nor might she act as midwife to an alien idolatress, but she might be hired to do so to prevent enmity. An alien idolatress might act as midwife to a daughter of Israel and suckle her child but only in her presence to make sure that the idolatress would not destroy the child.

17. One was forbidden to do business with those who went to idolatrous revels, but when they came out one might deal with them unless they came out arm in arm as this meant they would go back again. One could deal with an Israelite going to such revels but when he returned it was not allowed as then he might have idolatrous money. With an apostate Israelite one might not deal either when he went in or came out.

18. One might not deal with an Israelite who had returned from an idolater's fair lest he had money from selling goods to an idolater there, for the proceeds of idolatry were not allowed to benefit the hand of an Israelite. Idolatrous money in the hand of an idolater was allowed and business might be done with a non-Jew returning from an idolater's fair but not with a Jew from such a fair. One might not deal with an apostate Israelite either when he went to or returned from such a fair.

TREATISE 4

Chapter 10

1. One was not allowed to make a treaty of peace with the seven Canaanite peoples that allowed them to go on worshipping idols, as the verse states: 'Thou shalt make no covenant with them' (Deuteronomy 7:2). They might either repent or might be destroyed. It was also forbidden to show them mercy; the verse continues, 'nor shew mercy unto them' and, if one saw one of them perishing or drowning in a river, one might not save him. If one saw him near to death one might not help, but to destroy him with one's own hand or push him into a pit or the like was forbidden unless he was at war with the Israelites. How did this apply to the seven Canaanite tribes? As regards traitors and unbelievers in Israel, the Law was to destroy them with one's own hand and put them in a pit of destruction because they oppressed Israel and turned the people from following the Lord.

2. From that you learn that it was forbidden to doctor idolaters even for hire, but if a doctor was afraid of a person or general enmity, he might doctor for pay, never for nothing. The stranger in our midst might be treated for nothing because we were commanded to help him to live.

3. Houses and fields in the land of Israel might not be sold to idolaters but in Syria houses might be sold to them but not fields. In Israel, houses might be rented to them on condition that they did not set up a settlement. A settlement consisted of not less than three houses. Fields might not be leased to them in Israel but might be in Syria. Why was a field important? For two reasons, first, the idolater paid no tithes, and second he might settle on the land. It was allowed to sell them both houses and fields outside Israel because that was not the land of Israel.

4. However, where it was permitted to lease a house, permission to dwell in it might not be given because idols would then be brought into it, as the verse says: 'Neither shalt thou bring an abomination into thine house' (Deuteronomy 7:26), but houses could be leased as stores. One might not sell to an idolater fruit or grain which was still on the stalk, but might sell it to one on condition that he harvested it; the purchase was then binding. Why was one forbidden to sell to idolaters? Because it is written: 'Nor shew mercy unto them' (Deuteronomy 7:2), which means not to allow them to settle in the land of Israel, and, if they had no land, any settlement had to be temporary. One was also forbidden to

praise them, even to say how beautiful an idol was. How much more was it forbidden to speak in praise of their deeds and utterances of devotion. The verse above states: 'Nor shew mercy unto them'. They might not find grace in thine eyes because after becoming attached to them one might learn the evils of idolatry. One might not make a free gift to them but one might give to an alien[1] since the verse states: 'unto the stranger that is in thy gates, that he may eat it or thou mayest sell unto an alien' (Deuteronomy 14:21), implying selling to an alien, but not presenting it.

5.　　Relief was given to poor idolaters in the same way as it was given to poor Israelites — for the sake of peace. Poor idolaters were not prevented from gathering gleanings and an overlooked sheaf in the corner of a field, and that also was for the sake of peace. Even on their festival days they were greeted as this contributed to peace but a greeting was never uttered twice. One might not enter an idolater's house on his festival to give a greeting. If one met him in the market, one greeted him quietly and respectfully.

6.　　All these courtesies were exchanged only at a time when Israel was in exile among idolaters or an idolatrous power was holding the land of Israel. When Israel had the power in her own land it was forbidden to allow idolatrous settlements. Sojourners were not allowed in the land of Israel and traders going from place to place might not travel in the land unless they had accepted the seven commandments of Noah?[2] The verse says: 'They shall not dwell in thy land' (Exodus 23:33), not even for an hour. If an idolater did accept the seven commands of Noah, he was an alien settled in the land. Such alien residents were acceptable in a jubilee year; at other times only proselytes were accepted.

Chapter 11

1.　　It was forbidden to follow the customs of idolaters or to copy their dress or hair styles, as the verse says: 'And ye shall not walk in the manners of the nation, which I cast out

---

[1] There seem to have been several categories of 'stranger' from time to time: ger meant an alien; ger toshav, a stranger who was not an idol worshipper and who accepted the seven commandments of Noah's people; ger zedek, a righteous alien, an accepted proselyte of Judaism.

[2] Of the seven commandments accepted in Noah's time six were negative — against blaspheming, idolatry, incest, murder, robbery and the eating of part of a living animal. The one positive command was to set up some local system of government.

before you' (Leviticus 20:23). 'Neither shall ye walk in their ordinances' (Leviticus 13:3). 'Take heed to thyself that thou be not snared by following them' (Deuteronomy 12:30). All these verses have one meaning, namely to warn one not to be like unto them. An Israelite should be separated from idolaters and recognised by his dress and other things, just as he is separated in knowledge and understanding. It was said: 'and have severed you from other people, that ye should be Mine' (Leviticus 20:26). An Israelite might not wear any garment especially used by idolaters, or grow tufts of hair on the head as they did, nor might he shave the sides and leave the locks at the back of his head as they did in what was called a queue, nor shave the hair of his face from ear to ear, nor leave locks behind as they did. An Israelite might not build edifices resembling those of idolaters, which brought people together. Anyone doing these things or the like was flogged.

2.   When an Israelite was cutting an idolater's hair he should refrain from cutting the hair within three fingers of his queue.

3.   An Israelite holding royal office close to the king and having to sit with councillors, if he was embarrassed at being unlike them, was allowed to dress as they did and so appear correct in the king's presence.

4.   It was forbidden to consult omens as idolaters did. The verse says: 'Neither shall ye use enchantment' (Leviticus 19:26). What were these omens? An example is when a person says 'because the bread fell out of my mouth or the stick fell out of my hand, I shall not go to such and such a place today for, if I go, I shall not be successful' or 'because a fox passed on my right hand, I shall not leave my doorstep today for, if I do, I shall meet a cheat'. Another example is when someone on hearing the chirp of a bird says that something will or will not happen, or that it will be good to do so and so and bad to do something else. Some have said 'kill that cock which crows in the evening or that hen which crows like a cock'. Others, like Eliezer servant of Abraham act on self-chosen signs saying, 'if such and such happens to me I shall do so and so, and if it does not happen, I shall not do it'. All such practices were forbidden and those who offended were striped.

5.   Further examples are those who said 'this dwelling which I built gave good fortune, and this wife whom I married, or this animal that I bought was a blessing because

since then I have become rich'. However, if one asked a child 'what verse are you learning?' and was told that it was a verse from the Blessings and he might rejoice and say 'that is a good omen', this was allowed because future actions were not influenced or prevented. To refer to past actions was allowed.

6.   Who was a practitioner of divination? He who occupied himself with useless actions to divert attention from ordinary events and at the same time predicted future happenings, saying that so and so will happen or will not happen, or that one ought to do such and such a thing, or warn against it. Some fortune tellers manipulated sand or stones, some fell to the ground exhausted and cried out, and some looked into an iron, mirror or lamp and saw imaginary things. Some took a stick in the hand and leaned on it and knocked until their thoughts were diverted and then spoke. This was what was meant when the prophet said: 'My people ask counsel at their stocks, and their staff declareth unto them' (Hosea 4:12).

7.   It was forbidden to practise such augury or to consult soothsayers. Anyone who did so was given a 'rebel's beating', but the soothsayer himself, when he did such things, was lashed, as the verse says: 'There shall not be found among you anyone ... that useth divination' (Deuteronomy 18:10).

8.   Who were the observers of the times? They were those who predicted by astrology that one day was good or bad, one day suitable for some work and one year or month bad for something.

9.   It was forbidden to be an observer of times, even if no action was involved. Astrologers deceived fools who thought their utterances were true and wise. All who followed them and arranged work or travelling by the times of the stars were striped, as the verse says: 'nor observe times' (Leviticus 19:26). Similarly anyone who deluded the eyes by conjuring or by sleight of hand alleging it to be wonderful was included among observers of the times and his punishment was stripes.

10.   Who was a charmer? One who uttered unintelligent words which the people thought in their ignorance meant something useful. Some of these said that words pronounced over a snake or scorpion would remove danger or that words spoken to a fire would prevent damage. Other charmers while talking held a key, or stone or such like in their hands. All of these were forbidden. The charmer himself who held anything in his hand or did anything as he spoke [1], even pointing

---

[1] There was a great emphasis on the importance of action, the deed, in Israelite tradition.

103

with a finger, was striped, as the verse states: 'There shall not be found among you ... a charmer, or a consulter with familiar spirits, or a wizard, or a necromancer' (Deuteronomy 18:10-11). If an astrologer just muttered, did not move a finger or his head and had nothing in his hand, anyone before him listening and appearing to enjoy it was whipped as a rebel, because he shared in his folly. All such mutterings and indecent pronouncements, although harmless, did no good.

11.   If anyone was bitten by a scorpion or a snake, the bitten spot could be charmed, even on the Sabbath, to compose his mind and strengthen his heart. Although this was not of use, it was allowed because the person was in danger and might take leave of his senses.

12.   Anyone who whispered over a wound or read a verse of the Torah over a child to prevent him being afraid, or put a scroll of the Law or phylacteries on a child to make him sleep was not regarded as a sorcerer or magician; but such denied the Torah by using it to heal the body when it is really for a spiritual healing, even as the verse states: 'So shall they be life unto thy soul' (Proverbs 3:22). A healthy person who read verses from the Torah or Psalms so that righteousness might be imputed to him and that he might be protected from evil and accidents was allowed to do so.

13.   Who were the necromancers? Some starved and went to live in a cemetery so that the dead might come to them in a dream and reveal what they asked for. Others dressed themselves in special garments and spoke special words and burned incense and slept alone so that the dead might come before them and speak to them in a dream. In general, all who did something in order that a dead person might appear with information were striped. The verse says: 'There shall not be found among you a necromancer' to question the dead (Deuteronomy 18:10-11).

14.   It was forbidden to consult the dead or familiar spirits, as the above verse states: 'There shall not be found among you ... a consulter with familiar spirits'. Learn from this that one who practises spiritualism deserved to be stoned. Anyone who sought a necromancer was warned and given a rebel's beating. If he joined in the ceremony and did as he was told, he was striped.

15.   A charmer deserved to be stoned if he practised magic, but if he merely deluded the eyes by make-believe action, he was just beaten as a rebel. The negative command 'Thou shalt not suffer a witch to live' was one which did not need a

warning before the death sentence was pronounced by the *Beth Din.*

16. All these practices are deceitful and false and they led the ancient idolaters of many lands astray and many became accustomed to follow them. It is not worthy of Israelites who are truly of the wise to be attached to such follies or to imagine that they are beneficial, as the verse says: 'Surely there is no enchantment against Jacob, neither is there any divination against Israel' (Numbers 23:23), and again, 'For these nations, which thou shalt possess, hearkened unto observers of times, and unto diviners: but as for thee, the Lord thy God hath not suffered thee so to do' (Deuteronomy 18:14). All who believe in these and similar practices and think in their hearts that they are true and wise, although forbidden by the Torah, are merely foolish and ignorant, most are in general women and children of imperfect knowledge. But those who are wise and perfect in knowledge know clearly that all such practices forbidden in the Torah are not wise but are vain and foolish and are followed only by those who lack knowledge and abandon the ways of truth altogether because of them. On this account the Torah warns against all these follies, and say: 'Thou shalt be perfect[1] with the Lord thy God (Deuteronomy 18:13).

Chapter 12

1. It was forbidden to shave the sides of the head as the idolaters did. The verse says: 'Ye shall not round the corners of your heads' (Leviticus 19:27), and one was counted guilty for each side. So anyone who shaved both sides, even at the same time and after being warned, was striped twice. Whether he shaved the sides only and left the rest of the head or shaved the whole head, he was flogged, because he had shaved the sides. That applied to a shaver but the person shaved was not striped unless he had helped the barber. Anyone who cut off the corners of the hair of a child was striped.

2. A woman barber who cut off the corners of a man's hair was not guilty as the verse states: 'Ye shall not round the corners of your heads, neither shalt thou mar the corners of thy beard' (Leviticus 19:27). Therefore whosoever is concerned with destroying the beard is also concerned with rounding off the corners of the hair; a woman, as she has no

1 Faultless or sincere.

beard, is not concerned with rounding the corners. Manservants having beards were also forbidden to round their heads.

3. Negative commands in the Torah applied to both men and women except those about not cutting the beard and rounding the hair, and a priest's contamination by a dead body which refers only to men. Positive commands, which applied only at certain times and were not frequent, women were exempt from, except for the prayer of sanctification of the Sabbath, the eating of unleavened bread on the night of Passover, eating the Paschal Lamb, and its slaughter, being present when all Israel assembled once in seven years and rejoicing on the festivals which are obligatory for women.

4. Hermaphrodites, who have neither the form of a man nor of a woman, were obliged to fulfil all commands but, if one of them transgressed, no lashings were given.

5. Although a woman might shave the corners of her head, she was not allowed to do that to a man or even to a child.

6. As to the hair locks left at the corners of the head, the sages gave no instructions but we did hear from our elders that they might not be less than forty hairs and one was allowed to cut them with clippers because the prohibition only applied to their destruction with a razor.

7. It was the custom of idolatrous priests to destroy their beards and because of that the Torah forbade it. There are five corners of a beard: the upper cheek, the lower cheek on the right and left, and the long part. One was striped for destroying these corners and if one destroyed all five, one was striped five times. There was no guilt unless one shaved with a razor, for the verse says: 'Neither shalt thou mar the corners of thy beard' (Leviticus 19:27). So if one clipped the beard with scissors, he was not guilty. One who was shaved was not guilty unless he helped in the work. A woman was allowed to destroy her beard if she had hair on her chin and if she shaved a man's beard she was not guilty.

8. One was allowed to shave a moustache with a razor, that was hair on the upper lip or hair hanging from the lower lip. Although this was allowed, it was not a custom in Israel but a moustache was trimmed if it was an inconvenience while eating and drinking.

9. Removal of hair from other parts of the body, such as from the axillae and genital region, was not forbidden in the Torah but the scribes forbade it and anyone doing so was beaten as a rebel. How did this apply? In a place where it was

only practised by women the prohibition prevented men from acting like women. However, in a place where both men and women followed the practice, the men were not liable to punishment. It was permitted to remove hair from other regions of the body with clippers.

10. A woman might not adorn herself as a man by putting on a turban or helmet on her head or dress in armour and so on, or shave her head like a man. Nor might a man adorn himself like a woman dressing in gaudy clothes and golden ornaments in a place where according to local custom only women wore them. A man adorned as a woman or a woman adorned as a man was striped. Any man who plucked out white hairs among the dark ones of his head or beard was striped and was guilty after he pulled out the first hair because he was behaving as a women. If he dyed his hair dark, after dyeing one white hair, he was striped. A hermaphrodite was not allowed to wrap up his head like a women or shave it like a man, but if he did either of the two he was not striped.

11. The tattooing mentioned in the Torah was the practice of making incisions on the body and filling these with sand, ink or other dyes which left marks. It was the custom of people who tattooed themselves for idolatry to announce that they were slaves sold to an idol and marked for its service. As soon as anyone was tattooed on any part of the body, they were striped, whether a man or a woman. One who just wrote or just painted on a dye, but did not tattoo with a dye, was not guilty. The verse says: 'Ye shall not make any cuttings in your flesh for the dead, nor print any marks upon you' (Leviticus 19:28). How did this apply? To one who did tattooing, but the person tattooed was not responsible unless he had assisted in the work. If he had not contributed to it, he was not striped.

12. Anyone who made a single cut on himself for the dead was striped. The verse above applied both to a priest or layman. If one made one incision for five dead or five incisions for one dead, one was striped five times, provided due warning had been given each time.

13. Cutting and tattooing were alike and just as idolaters cut their flesh for the dead in their distress, so they wounded themselves before their idols. The verse states: 'And they cried aloud, and cut themselves after their manner with knives and lancets' (I Kings 18:28). This was forbidden by the Torah where it says: 'Ye shall not cut yourselves for the

dead' (Deuteronomy 14:1). If it is over the dead, it did not matter whether it was done by hand or with a tool, the doer was striped. If done for an idol with an instrument, one was culpable and was striped, but one was excused if the hand only had been used.

14. Included in this warning about cutting is another that there should not be two courts of justice in one city, one following one custom and the other another custom, because such a state of affairs leads to great divisions. When the verse states: 'Ye shall not cut[1] yourselves', the rabbis interpreted this as meaning you shall not cut yourselves into groups.

15. One who made himself entirely bald for the dead was striped. The verse says: 'nor make any baldness between your eyes[2] for the dead' (Deuteronomy 14:1). Whether it was a lay Israelite or a priest who made himself bald for the dead it was the same and he was striped once. One who made four or five bald patches for the dead person was striped according to the number of patches, if he had been warned as he made each one, whether they were made with his hand, or by poison, or he had dipped his fingers in poison and left it in five places on his head. Although he may have had only one warning, he was striped five times because they were all made at the same time. One was guilty wherever it was done, on the head or between the eyes. The verse states: 'They shall not make baldness upon their head' (Leviticus 21:5). And how big might the bald place be? As big as the size of a groat which appeared free of hair.

16. Anyone who made a bald patch on his head or cut his flesh, because his house had fallen down or his ship had sunk was excused and was not lashed because that applied only when it was done over a death or in the service of idols. If one made baldness on his friend's head or tattooed his body and the friend helped, so long as this was deliberate, both were striped. If one did it in ignorance and the other deliberately, the former was excused and the other striped.

Here ends the treatise on Idolatry.

---

[1] A word with a double meaning.
[2] Forehead.

Treatise 5
REPENTANCE

This deals with one positive commandment that the sinner shall repent of his guilt and confess it before the Lord. The explanation of this command and the principles related to it are given in this treatise.

Chapter 1

1.   If a man trangresses one of the positive or negative commands of the Torah, whether intentionally or by mistake, when he repents and turns back from the sin it is a duty to confess before the Lord — blessed be He! The verse states: 'When a man or woman shall commit any sin ... they shall confess their sin which they have done' (Numbers 5: 6,7) and this is a confession in words and the confession is a positive command. How is it done? The sinner says: 'I beseech Thee Great Name, I have sinned. I have been perverse and transgressed before thee, I have done so and so. Now behold! I repent and am ashamed of my deed and I shall not repeat it again'. This is the fundamental form of confession. Whoever elaborates his confession and prolongs it is praiseworthy.   But the transgressor or guilty one when bringing sacrifices for mistakes or deliberate misdeeds will not be pardoned by a sacrifice until he repents and confesses in words, as the verse says: 'he shall confess that he hath sinned' (Leviticus 5:5). Also all under sentence of death from the *Beth Din* and those sentenced to lashings do not atone by death or the lashing unless they repent and confess. Anyone who injures his fellow man or damages him in money matters, even if he makes recompence for what is due, does not have atonement until he has confessed and turned from such doings for ever. As the verse states: 'Any sin that men commit ... they shall confess their sin which they have done' (Numbers 5:6,7).

2.   The scapegoat because it is sent away atones for the sins of all Israel. The High Priest confesses over it for the whole of Israel. As the verse says: 'Aaron shall ... confess him all the iniquities of the children of Israel' (Leviticus 16:21). The scapegoat atones for all the transgressions mentioned in the

Torah, the minor and major, the deliberate or accidental and whether done knowingly or in ignorance. The goat atones for all who repent, but if the sinner does not repent, the goat only atones for minor offences. What are minor and major transgresstions? The major sins are those which carry the death penalty of the *Beth Din* or *karet* (see glossary). False swearing, although it does not imply *karet*, is a major sin. All other negative and positive commands which do not involve *karet* are minor.

3. In these times when there is no Temple standing and we have no altar for atonement, there is nothing left but repentance. Repentance atones for all transgressions. Even one who has done evil all his days, if he repents, will have nothing of his wickedness held against him in the end. The verse says: 'As for the wickedness of the wicked, he shall not fall thereby in the day that he turneth from his wickedness' (Ezekiel 33:12). The Day of Atonement *(Yom Kippur)* itself atones for those who repent, even as the verse states: 'For on that day shall the priest make an atonement for you' (Leviticus 16:30).

4. Although repentance atones for everything and the Day of Atonement itself atones, there are some transgressions which are atoned for at once and there are others which are not forgiven for some time. For example, if a man sins against a positive commandment which does not carry *karet* and he repents, he is forgiven straight away; of such the verse says: 'Return ye backsliding children, and I will heal your backslidings' (Jeremiah 3:22). If he transgresses a negative command which does not deserve *karet* or the death penalty of the *Beth Din* and he repents, it is suspended till the Day of Atonement pardons; of such the verse says: 'For on that day shall the priest make an atonement for you' (Leviticus 16:30). If he sinned and deserved *karet* or execution from the *Beth Din,* repentance and the Day of Atonement suspends them and the sufferings which follow for him complete the atonement. Forgiveness and atonement are not complete until suffering comes to him; of such it is said: 'Then will I visit their transgressions with the rod, and their iniquity with stripes' (Psalm 89:32). When does this apply? To one who does not profane the Holy Name when he has sinned. But he who blasphemed the Holy Name, even if he repented and was still penitent on the Day of Atonement and suffering came to him, is not completely forgiven until his death. Repentance and the Day of Atonement and suffering

may suspend judgment but only death atones, as the verse says: 'Surely this iniquity shall not be purged from you till ye die' (Isaiah 22:14).

Chapter 2

1. What is a complete repentance? When one has the opportunity to repent a transgression but does not repeat it because of repentance, and not on account of fear or lack of strength. For example, a man who knew a woman sinfully and after a time met her again alone and he still loved her and is still strong and they meet in the same place, if he turns aside and sins not, he has attained complete repentance. Of such Solomon said: 'Remember now thy Creator in the days of thy youth' (Ecclesiastes 12:1). If a man does not repent except in old age when it is impossible to repeat what he has done, that is not the highest repentance, but it is of use and he is a penitent. Even if he has sinned all his life and repents on the day of his death and he dies penitent, all his sin is forgiven. As the verse says: 'While the sun, or the light, or the moon, or the stars be not darkened, nor the clouds return after rain' (Ecclesiastes 12:2). This means the day of death, and, if he remembers his Creator before it, he is forgiven.
2. What is repentance? It is that the sinner shall desert his wrong doing, remove it from his thoughts and determine in his heart not to do it again, as the verse states: 'Let the wicked forsake his way' (Isaiah 55:7). So he shall repent for the transgression, as was said: 'Surely after that I was turned, I repented' (Jeremiah 31:19). He should call 'Him who knows all secrets' to witness that he will never return to the sin, as the verse says: 'neither will we say any more to the work of our hands, Ye are our gods' (Hosea 14:3). It is necessary to make confession with the lips and to utter the matters about which the heart is determined.
3. Anyone who confesses something verbally and does not determine to abandon it is like someone who immerses himself for purification and holds a reptile[1] in his hand; for he knows that the immersion will be of no use until he has thrown the creeping thing away. Of such the verse says: 'whoso confesseth and forsaketh his sins shall have mercy' (Proverbs 28:13). It is necessary to specify the sin, as was said: 'Oh, this people have sinned a great sin, and have made them gods of gold' (Exodus 32:31).

[1] Meaning an unclean thing.

111

4.   Among the ways of repenting the penitent should cry continually before the Lord with tears and supplications, do charitable deeds according to his ability and isolate himself completely from the sin which he committed; and he may change his name as if to say 'I am another person, not the man who did those things'. He changes his conduct and does good according to the path of right. He may leave his home because exile atones for evil as it leads to humility and a lowly spirit.

5.   It is praiseworthy if the penitent confesses before others and makes known his transgression to them and reveals the sin between himself and his neighbour to others and says: 'Indeed, I did wrong to someone, I did so and so and today I repent and am sorry'. The arrogant, who do not let the sin be known but cover it up, are not truly repentant, as the verse says: 'He that covereth his sins shall not prosper' (Proverbs 28:13). In what circumstances does this apply? To the transgressions which are between a man and his fellow men. But it is not necessary to publicise the transgressions which are between man and the Most High; indeed it is presumptuous to reveal them. One should repent before the Lord — blessed be He! — and enumerate the sins before Him, and make public confession in general terms by merely stating, 'I have sinned'. It is well for him not to reveal these sins, as the verse says: 'Blessed is he whose transgression is forgiven, whose sin is covered' (Psalm 32:1).

6.   Although repentance and crying out are always good they are better in the ten days between the New Year's Day (Rosh-ha Shqnah) and the Day of Atonement, for then they are accepted at once, as the verse says: 'Seek ye the Lord while he may be found' (Isaiah 55:6). To whom does this apply? To the individual. In the community when there is confession and loud lamentation with a full heart they are answered, as the verse says: 'the Lord our God is in all things that we call upon him for' (Deuteronomy 4:7).

7.   The Day of Atonement is the time set apart for repentance for all, the individual and the community and the aim is forgiveness and pardon for Israel. Therefore it is the duty of all to repent and confess on that day. The command for the Day of Atonement is for the first confession to be on the previous evening [1] before the meal, so that one may not choke on the food before confession. Although confession

[1] The Jewish day starts at sundown for 'the evening and the morning were the first day' (Genesis 1:5).

112

is made before the evening meal, it is repeated in the night of the Day, at the morning prayer, and evening prayer, the additional prayer and the closing prayer. And when is confession made? By the individual after his *Amida* prayer (see glossary) and by the leader of the community half way through the repetition of the *Amida* after the fourth benediction.

8.   The confession of all Israel is 'We have all sinned' and that is the fundamental form of confession. Confession of sins on the Day of Atonement should be repeated on Days of Atonement in following years, although one remains penitent, for it is said: 'I acknowledge my transgressions and my sin is ever before me' (Psalm 51:3).

9.   Repentance on the Day of Atonement atones only for those sins that are between man and the Most High, for example, eating forbidden food or having forbidden intercourse and such like. But sins which are between man and his fellow men, such as injuring or cursing, or robbing him and such like, are never pardoned until he makes restitution and appeases his fellow. Even if he returns money which is owed, he must appease and ask for pardon. Even if he has only provoked his neighbour in words, he must make peace and entreat him until he forgives. If his friend is not willing to forgive him, he must bring a group of three neighbours to appease him. If he still refuses, a second or third group should be brought and, if they are refused, he should be left. For then the sin of refusing to forgive rests on him. But if it was his master or his Rabbi, he must ask forgiveness a thousand times until he is forgiven.

10.   A man is forbidden to be cruel and must be conciliatory; he should be easily appeased, hard to make angry and, when a wrongdoer begs his forgiveness, he ought to forgive with a whole heart and willing spirit. Even if he was persecuted and much wronged, he ought not to be vengeful and bear a grudge, because such is the way of the upright hearts of the children of Israel. The idolaters' hard hearts are not so and their anger holds for ever. So it was concerning the Gibeonites; because they were unforgiving and not conciliatory, it was said of them: 'now the Gibeonites were not of the children of Israel' (2 Samuel 21:2).

11.   One who sins against his friend and the friend dies before forgiveness is sought should bring ten men and stand at his grave and say to them: 'I have sinned against the God of Israel and my friend and have done thus to him'. If he

owed money it should be returned to the inheritors; if they are not known it should be left with the *Beth Din* with a confession.

Chapter 3

1.   Every human being possesses virtues and vices and he whose virtues are greater than his vices is a righteous man; he whose vices are greater than his virtues is wicked; when vices and virtues are equal he is intermediate. A country is similar. If the virtues of its inhabitants are greater than their vices the state is just; and if their vices are greater than their virtues it is wicked. So it is in all the world.

2.   A man whose evil doings are greater than his virtues dies prematurely in his evil, as the verse says: 'For the multitude of thine iniquity' (Hosea 9:7). Similarly a state in which evil predominates is destroyed prematurely, as the verse says: 'Because the cry of Sodom and Gomorrah is great' (Genesis 18:20). So it is in all the world. If the evil exceeds the good, the evil ones are destroyed prematurely, as was said: 'God saw that the wickedness of man was great in the earth' (Genesis 6:5). The reckoning in this is not according to the number of virtues and vices but according to their magnitude. There is virtue which overbalances much vice, even as the verse says: 'because in him there is found some good thing' (I Kings 14:13). And there is an evil which over-balances much good, as the verse says: 'One sinner destroy-eth much good' (Ecclesiastes 9:18). No one weighs these things except the all-knowing Lord; it is He who knows the balance of good and evil.

3.   Anyone who regrets a good deed which he has done and doubts the value of good deeds and says in his heart: 'What do I benefit by doing them? I wish I had not done them', truly he utterly destroys them all and no memory of any of his virtues remains, as the verse says: 'The righteousness of the righteous shall not deliver him in the day of his trans-gression' (Ezekiel 33:12). This can only apply to one who doubts the value of his former good deeds. In the same way as virtue and vice in man are weighed at the hour of death, so every year the evil of every man born on earth is weighed to find his worth on the festival of the New Year. He who is found righteous is recorded for life and he who is found wicked is sealed for death, and for him who is intermediate judgment is suspended until the Day of Atonement when if he repents he is sealed for life and if not for death.

4.   Although blowing the ram's horn on the festival of the
New Year is a scriptural decree, it is symbolic as if saying
'Awake ye sleepers from your sleep; and slumberers arise
from your slumbering, examine your deeds and turn in
repentance and remember your Creator. All who forget the
truth in the futilities of the times and err all their years in
vanities and emptiness which cannot benefit or save, look to
your lives, improve your ways and deeds and let each one
abandon his evil ways and bad thoughts'. Therefore it is
necessary for each man to regard himself all the year round as
balanced between innocence and guilt. Similarly the whole
world is balanced between innocence and guilt. If a sinner
sins, he may bring down himself and all the world on the side
of guilt and so cause destruction. He who observes a precept
may bring himself and the whole world onto the side of
virtue, and so gain salvation and deliverance for himself and
them, as the verse says: 'the righteous is an everlasting
foundation' (Proverbs 10:25). Thus the righteous one inclines
all the world to virtue and rescues it. Because of this all the
people of Israel are accustomed to be diligent in charity and
good conduct and the observance of precepts from the
festival of the New Year to the Day of Atonement more than
at any other time in the year. It was also customary to stay
up all night during those ten days and to pray in the
synagogue with supplication and humility until the day
dawns.
5.   At the hour when the vices and virtues of a man are
weighed, neither the first nor the second time of sinning is
considered but his sins are counted from the third time
onwards. If it is found that the vices exceed the virtues from
the third onwards, then the two first are added and they are
all judged. If it is found that the virtues balance the vices
from the third vice onwards, then all the previous iniquities
are wiped out. Then the third sin counts as the first, for the
first two are forgiven already. Similarly the fourth becomes
the first because the third is cancelled, and so on to the end.
When does this apply? To the individual. The verse says:
'Lo, all these things worketh God oftentimes with man, to
bring back his soul from the pit, to be enlightened with the
light of the living' (Job 33:29,30). But in the community the
first, second and third iniquities are suspended even as it was
said: 'For three transgressions of Israel, and for four, I will
not turn away the punishment thereof' (Amos 2:6). Therefore when the reckoning comes it applies from the fourth

sin onwards. When it comes to sins in the middle grade, such as not wearing their phylacteries, then each case is judged on its own and they still have a share in the world to come! Similarly all the wicked whose vices are many are judged according to their sins and they have a share in the world to come because all Israel has a share in it although they have sinned. The verse says: 'Thy people also shall be all righteous; they shall inherit the land for ever' (Isaiah 60:21). Land is an allegory here, meaning the land of the living which is the world to come, and the pious of all nations have a share in that world.

6.   These are they who have no share in the world to come, who are cut off and destroyed and are judged on account of great wickedness and sins forever and ever. Heretics, atheists and those who reject the Torah and deny the resurrection and the coming of a Messiah and the apostate. Also those who cause many to sin and those who separate themselves from the congregation, those who sin with a high hand in public like Jehoiakim (2 Kings 23:36—24:6), also informers and those who spread fear among the people, other than fear of the Lord, those who shed blood, those who are slanderers and those who abolish circumcision.

7.   There are five categories of heretics: (1) he who says there is no God and the universe has no leader, (2) he who says there is a leader but there are two or more, (3) he who says there is a Master but that he has a body and form, (4) he who says that there is a Master but he is not the first cause and basis of everything, and (5) he who worships a star or planet and the like and holds such to be intermediaries between himself and the Lord of the Universe. Every one of these five is a heretic.

8.   There are three categories of atheists, (1) one who says there is no prophecy in Israel and that no knowledge from the Creator reaches the heart of man, (2) one who denies the prophecy of Moses our teacher, (3) one who says the Creator does not know about man's actions. Every one of these three is an atheist. There are three categories of those who refuse to accept the Torah: (1) those who say that it is not from

[1] The share is never defined. Sometimes it seems to mean length of days in this world, and at other times the life of the Spirit after death. The idea of personal immortality arose during times of great persecution but was never accepted by the Sadducees as a due for misery. Maimonides seems to suggest that the share in the world to come depended upon some contribution to the future of all mankind as well as to Israel.

God; even if they say that one verse or word was spoken by
Moses on his own, they deny the Torah, (2) he who denies
the oral tradition and its preachers as did the Sadducees
Zadok and Bythos, (3) he who says that the Creator changed
one commandment to another and that the Torah is
suspended, although it came from the Lord. All these three
deny the Torah.

9.   There are two kinds of apostasy in Israel: (1) one who
rejects a single command, and (2) one who rejects the Torah
altogether. He who is apostate against one command and
determines to transgress it intentionally and becomes accustomed to do so publicly, even if it is a minor command such
as dressing himself always in clothes of mixed wool and flax
or cutting the edges of his hair, as if he could abolish a
command forever, he is an apostate if he does it deliberately.
An example of one who rejects the whole Torah is he who
turns to idolatry at the time of persecution and says 'What
benefit is it to me to stick to Israel when they are down and
persecuted? It is better for me to side with the powerful'. He
has rejected the whole Torah.

10.   Who are those who cause others to sin? For example
one who commits a major sin like that which Jeroboam,
Zadok and Bythos did; or one who commits a minor sin, even
annulling one positive command; or one who forces others
to transgress like Manasseh, who slew the children of Israel
when they would not serve idols; or one who misleads others
and causes them to stray.

11.   A dissenter from the ways of the community, although
he does not transgress but separates himself from the congregation of Israel, and does not perform duties at all, does
not share in their distresses or fasts but goes his own way like
the rest of the people in the land and behaves as if he was not
one of the children of Israel; such has no share in the world
to come. One who sins with a high hand like Jehoiakim
(2 Kings 23:36) whether the transgressions are minor or
major has no share in the world to come; and of such it was
said: 'He who misinterprets the Torah with a brazen face and
is not ashamed to disobey the Torah'.

12.   There are two types of informers. One who gives evidence against his neighbour to a non-Jew in order to destroy
or crush him, and one who informs against his neighbour so
that his money be turned over to an idolater or to a robber.
Both these types have no share in the world to come.

13.   Those who cause terror among the public, and who

oppress the community with force and make it full of fear and dread to gain honour for themselves, and not for the glory of God, such are idolatrous rulers.

14. These twenty-four types of which we have spoken, even those among the people of Israel, have no share in the world to come; but there are also lesser transgressions about which the sages said that he who makes a regular practice of them will have no share in the world to come and that it was important to keep clear of them and to be warned against them. These are the types; one who denigrates his friend and gives him a bad name and shames him in public, glorifying himself by dishonouring his neighbour; one who shames scholars and his teachers and scorns holy feasts or profanes holy objects. Such have no share in the world to come if they die without repentance. But, if such a one repents of his evil and dies, he is a penitent and so belongs to the children of the world to come. There is nothing to stand in the way of repentance. Even a man who has been fundamentally an atheist all his days, if he repents at the last, has a share in the world to come, for the verse says: 'Peace, peace to him that is far off, and to him that is near, saith the Lord, and I will heal him' (Isaiah 57:19). All evil men, apostates and such like, who return in repentance publicly or in secret are accepted, as the verse says: 'Return ye backsliding children' (Jeremiah 3:22). One who is still a backslider but is secretly repentant and not in public, he is accepted as a penitent.

Chapter 4

1. There are twenty-four matters which impede repentance and four of these are great evils. If a man commits one of them the Holy One — blessed be He! — does not give the opportunity for repentance because of the gravity of the sin. These are the four great evils. (1) One who corrupts many; included in this category of evil is one who prevents people from performing a commandment. (2) One who leads his companion away from the path of good towards evil, for example by seduction and enticement. (3) One who sees that his son is committing evil deeds and does not rebuke him. Since his son is in his charge and, if he had corrected him, he might have separated him from sin, it is as if he himself had caused him to sin. Included in this is one who has the power to prevent others, whether individuals or multitudes, from

doing wrong and does not do so leaving them to go astray.
(4) One who says 'I will sin and repent', he is similar to one
who says 'I shall sin and the Day of Atonment will atone'.
2.   Of the twenty-four there are five matters which prevent
repentance in one who does them, and these are they. (1)
One who separates himself from the community, because
when he repents he is not among them and has no right to
share with them in their righteousness.   (2) One who dis-
agrees with the opinions of the sages, because after separation
from them he cannot discern the way back to repentance.
(3) One who scorns precepts because they are despicable in
his eyes. If he does not do them, how can he have merit. (4)
One who insults his teachers. This brings about strife and
trouble as happened to Gehazi (2 Kings 4:5) at the time
when he was in trouble and could not find a teacher to guide
him in the way of Truth. (5) One who hates correction, for
there is no way open for him to repent. Correction leads to
repentance because, when transgressions are pointed out to a
man and shame him he repents, as it is written in the Torah:
'Remember, and forget not ... ye have been rebellious against
the Lord' (Deuteronomy 9:7) and 'the Lord hath not given
you an heart to perceive' (Deuteronomy 29:4), and 'O
foolish people and unwise' (Deuteronomy 32:6). Isaiah
rebuked Israel saying 'Ah sinful nation' (Isaiah 1:4), 'The ox
knoweth his owner' (Isaiah 1:3) and 'I knew that thou art
obstinate' (Isaiah 48:4). Similarly the Lord commanded him
to rebuke evildoers in the verse: 'Cry aloud, spare not' (Isaiah
58:1). In the same way prophets rebuked Israel until they
returned in repentance. That is why it is necessary to appoint
in every community in Israel a sage, an old man who has
feared heaven since youth, who is beloved and who corrects
the people and leads them back to repentance. He who hates
correction does not come to the rebuker and listen to his
words but continues the sins that seem pleasing to him.
3.   Further there are five matters which make it impossible
to repent completely because they are between a man and
his fellow men and the sinner does not know whom he has
wronged, to whom to make amends and ask forgiveness.
(1) One who curses people in general and not one particular
person from whom he could ask forgiveness. (2) One who
goes shares with a thief and he does not know to whom the
stolen goods belong, because the thief steals from many and
comes and shares with him. In addition he strengthens the
thief's hand and causes him to sin. (3) One who finds lost

TREATISE 5

property and does not make it known so as to be able to
return it to its owner. Later when he repents he does not
know to whom it should be returned. (4) One who partakes
of part of an ox or anything belonging to the poor, or
orphans and widows. Such people are unfortunate, not
known publicly, and wander from city to city. No one knows
to whom the property belongs and to whom it should be
returned. (5) One who accepts a bribe to pervert justice; for
he does not know the extent of the perversion or how great
its power or if restitution could be made. Moreover the
matter has evil implications for it strengthens the hand of the
man who offers the bribe and causes him to sin.

4.   There are also five habits which if followed do not
encourage repentance, because they are little matters in the
eyes of most men and when performed are not thought of as
sin at all. (1) One who eats a meal when there is not enough
for the host himself. This is an offshoot of robbery and the
offender seems not to have sinned and says 'anyway I was
invited to eat'. (2) One who uses the pledge of a poor man
which may be but a hatchet or a plough. The offender says,
'there is no loss in this, I have not robbed him'. (3) One who
gazes with desire at a woman and imagines that it does not
matter and says 'have I seduced or gone near her?' He does
not know that such staring is a great evil and leads to immorality. The verse says: 'that ye seek not after your own heart
and your own eyes' (Numbers 15:39). (4) One who exalts
himself by denigrating his friend and says in his heart that
he is not sinning because his friend was absent and was not
shamed by the comparison of his good conduct and wisdom
with that of his friend, so that people would infer that he
was honourable and his friend despicable. (5) One who casts
suspicion on the upright and says in his heart that he has not
sinned. He says 'What have I done to him? What is there
except a suspicion that he did or did not do so and so?' He
does not realise that this is evil and that in his mind he has
placed an upright man among evildoers.

5.   Of the twenty four transgressions there are five which
lead a man to continue them always and make it hard for him
to abandon them. For that reason a man must be warned
about them that he should not stick to them, for these are
all very evil habits of mind. They are (1) slander, (2) an evil
tongue, (3) bad temper, (4) evil thought and (5) compan-
ionship with the wicked, for one learns his ways which
become imprinted on the heart. Of such Solomon said: 'He

120

that walketh with wise men shall be wise: but a companion of fools shall be destroyed' (Proverbs 13:20). We have explained already in the Treatise on Discernment the habits to which a man ought to accustom himself always. How much more should the penitent.

6. All these matters and what is related to them, although they obstruct repentance do not prevent it. If a man does turn away from them, he is a penitent and there is a share for him in the world to come.

Chapter 5

1. It is within the power of every man to incline himself to the path of good and to be righteous and the choice is his. If he wishes to go in the path of sin and become evil that is in his hand. This is what is written in the Torah: 'Behold the man is become as one of us, to know good and evil' (Genesis 3:22), that is to say that man as a species stands alone and there is no other like him in that man alone has the knowledge and understanding to recognise good and evil and does what he wishes; there is none to prevent him from doing good or evil. Because of this the verse said: 'Lest he put forth his hand and take also of the tree of life' (Genesis 3:22).

2. Do not imagine here what the silly Gentiles of the world and many of the foolish in Israel say that the Holy One — blessed be He! — decrees that every one from conception shall be righteous or wicked. The matter is not so. Each individual may become righteous like Moses, our master, or wicked like Jeroboam, wise or foolish, merciful or cruel, miserly or generous and similarly with all other attributes. There is no one to compel or order a man so as to draw him to one path or the other. He himself with his understanding inclines to the path which he chooses. Jeremiah said of this: 'Out of the mouth of the most High proceedeth not evil and good?' (Lamentations 3:38), which is to say that the Creator does not decree that a man be good or evil. Because of that the evildoer is spoiled by himself and it is necessary that he should weep and lament about his transgressions and what he has done to his spirit by serving it with evil. This is what the verse states: 'Wherefore doth a living man complain, a man for the punishment of his sins?' (Lamentations 3:39) and goes on because it is with our own will and understanding that we do evil. We must turn in penitence and desert our

wickedness, for the power is within our hands. Further the verse says: 'Let us search and try our ways, and turn again to the Lord' (Lamentations 3:40).

3.   This matter is an important principle and basis of the Torah and its precepts. The verse says: 'See, I have set before thee this day life and good, and death and evil' (Deuteronomy 30:15) and 'I call heaven and earth to record this day against you, that I have set before you life and death, blessing and cursing: therefore choose life, that both thou and thy seed may live' (Deuteronomy 30:19). This means that the choice of all that man wants to do, whether good or bad, is in your hands. On this the verse says: 'O, that there were such an heart in them, that they would fear Me, and keep all my commandments' (Deuteronomy 5:29). This means that the Creator does not compel the children of men and does not order them to do good or evil but hands the choice over to them.

4.   If the Lord had decreed that a man must be righteous or evil or if He had put something into man to direct him by inborn faculty to go in certain ways, or have special knowledge, and special understanding, or do special deeds, as the astrologers maintain in their foolish hearts, how could He, the Lord, have commanded us by the prophets to do this or not this? How could He command us to mend our ways and not follow wickedness if He had already decreed an inborn tendency from which one cannot deviate? What place would there be for the whole Torah and by what law and judgment could wickedness be punished or the righteous rewarded? 'Shall not the Judge of all the earth do right?' (Genesis 18:25). Do not be surprised and ask how can a man do what he chooses and have responsibility for his actions when nothing happens in the world without the permission of his Creator and His will. The verse states: 'Whatsoever the Lord pleased that did He in heaven, and in earth, in the seas, and all deep places' (Psalm 135:6). Know that all is in accord with His will although our actions are left to us. For example, just as the Creator desired the fire and the wind to fly upward, and the water and earth to go downward or the planet to go round in its circuit and all other creatures in the world to have the customs which He wished, so it was His will that man should have his own will and responsibility in his own hand, with his own understanding which the Lord gave allowing him to do all that man is able to do. Therefore man is judged according to his actions; if he does what is

good it benefits him and if he does evil it causes him evil. The prophets said of this: 'this hath been by your means' (Malachi 1:9) and also: 'they have chosen their own ways' (Isaiah 66:3). Solomon said about this: 'Rejoice, O young man, in thy youth ... but know thou, that for all these things God will bring thee into judgment' (Ecclesiastes 11:9). This is to say 'Know that the strength to do it is in your hand, and that in the future you will be judged'.

5.   You may ask: 'Does the Holy One — blessed be He! — not know all before it happens? Does He know that one will be just or wicked, or does He not know? If He knew that a man would be just, it would be impossible for that man not to be just. If He knows a man will be just but he turns out wicked, that shows He does not know clearly'. Know that the answer to these is longer in its measure than the world and broader than the sea; great depths and lofty heights are involved. But you must understand and know what I told you about it in the second chapter on Fundamentals of the Torah that the Holy One — blessed be He! — does not know of things outside Himself, like the children of man in whom being and knowledge are separate. He — blessed be His name! and His knowledge are one, and the mind of man cannot understand this about his Creator. In the same way it is not within the power of man to attain and reach the truth of the Creator, as the verse says: 'for there shall no man see me, and live' (Exodus 33:20). Similarly it is not within man's power to reach and find understanding of his Creator. This is what the prophet means in the words: 'For My thoughts are not your thoughts, neither are your ways My ways, saith the Lord' (Isaiah 55:8). Since this is so, it is not in our capacity to know how the Holy One — blessed be He! — knows all his creations and their doings, but it is known beyond doubt that the deeds of man are in his own hands, and the Holy One — blessed be He! — does not compel or decree how he acts. We know this not only because we have accepted the Law but by the clear evidence of words of wisdom. Therefore prophecy holds that man shall be judged according to his actions, whether they be good or bad. This is a fundamental principle upon which all the words of the prophets depend.

Chapter 6

1.   There are many verses in the Torah, and the words of the prophets that seem to contradict this basic belief and so

cause many to stumble and think that the Holy One —
blessed be He! — has decreed that man shall do good or evil
and that man's heart is not allowed to do as he wishes. So, I
shall explain to you here a great principle from which you
may know the interpretation of these verses. When a single
individual — or people of a country — sins intentionally and
deliberately, then they are liable to be punished, as we have
already said, and the Holy One — blessed be He! — knows
how to exact punishment. There is sin which Justice punishes
in this world, through the body or possessions or children:
for children have no understanding until they have reached
the age to observe the precepts[1] and are therefore regarded as
a man's property as it is written: 'Every man shall be put to
death for his own sin' (Deuteronomy 24:16). There is also a
sin for which justice demands punishment in the world to
come, and the sinner suffers no harm in this world. Further
there is a sin for which he is punished both in this world and
in the world to come.

2.   All these words apply at the time when a man has not
repented; but if he does repent that becomes a defence
against punishment. In the same way when a man sins
knowingly, he should repent conscientiously and of his own
free will.

3.   It is possible that a man might commit a grave iniquity
or many sins so that the sentence of the Judge of Truth
might be that the doer of those wrongs, done intentionally
and deliberately, would be denied repentance. As he might
not be given permission to repent of his wrong doing, and he
might die and perish in the iniquity which he did, of whom
the Holy One — blessed be He! — said through Isaiah: 'Make
the heart of this people fat ... and understand with their
heart, and convert, and be healed' (Isaiah 6:10), and again,
'But they mocked the messengers of God and despised his
words, and misused his prophets, until the wrath of the Lord
arose against his people, till there was no remedy' (2 Chronicles 36:16). This means that they sinned deliberately and
increased evils until it was necessary to deny them the repentance, which could have healed. Therefore it is written in
the Torah: 'I will harden Pharoah's heart' (Exodus 14:4),
because originally he sinned deliberately and did evil to
Israelites who were dwelling in his land. As the verse says:
'Come on, let us deal wisely with them' (Exodus 1:10).

[1] Judaism does not consider that a boy under 13 or a girl under 12
years is a responsible human being.

Justice demanded that repentance was denied him until he was punished. So the Holy One — blessed be He! — hardened Pharoah's heart. Why then did He send by Moses the message. 'Send out the people and repent', when the Holy One — blessed be He! — had already said to him: 'He will not send them' and 'But as for thee and thy servants, I know that ye will not yet fear the Lord God' (Exodus 9:30), and again, 'For this cause have I raised thee up' (Exodus 9:16), to make known to the people in the world that at the time when the Holy One refuses repentance to a sinner he cannot repent and dies in his sin which he did deliberately from the beginning. So also Sihon, on açcount of his sins, was rightly prevented from repenting. The verse says: 'The Lord thy God hardened his spirit, and made his heart obstinate' (Deuteronomy 2:30). Likewise also the Canaanites, on account of their horrible customs, were refused repentance until they engaged in battle with Israel. The verse says: 'For it was of the Lord to harden their heart, that they should come against Israel in battle, that He might destroy them utterly' (Joshua 11:20). So it was also with the people of Israel in the days of Elijah. Because they continued to sin, repentance was withheld from them, as the verse says: 'Thou hast turned their heart back again' (I Kings 18:37) which means repentance was withheld from them. Consequently it can be said, that the Lord did not decree Pharoah to do ill to Israel, or Sihon to sin in his country or the Canaanites to act horribly or the people of Israel to be idolatrous. All these sins were their own doing and consequently they deserved no opportunity to repent.

4. In this matter the pious ones and the prophets prayed to the Lord to help them to understand the path of Truth. as David said, 'Teach me thy way, O Lord; I will walk in thy truth' (Psalm 86:11). This means, 'allow not my sin to prevent me from the true path by which I would know Thy way and Unity of Thy Name'. Also in the verse 'and uphold me with thy free spirit' (Psalm 51:12), which means 'let my spirit do Thy will and let not my sin prevent repentance, so that I may be allowed to return and understand and know the way of Truth'. Similar verses can be interpreted in this way.

5. What does it mean when David said, 'Good and upright is the Lord: therefore will He teach sinners in the way. The meek will He guide in judgement: and the meek will He teach his way' (Psalm 25:8,9)? This refers to the prophets whom He sent to make the path of the Lord known and to turn

people back in repentance, and also to give them strength to learn and understand, because the character of man is such that if he follows the ways of wisdom and justice he longs for them and pursues them. This is what our teachers of blessed memory said, 'He who comes to be cleansed is helped', as if saying such a one will find himself aided in what he is striving for. But is it not written in the Torah that Israel would serve the Egyptians and be afflicted by them? This implies that God decreed that Egypt would do evil, also that Israel would arise and do evil and stray after the foreign gods of the country (Deuteronomy 31:16) implying a decree that Israel would worship idols. So why punish them? He did not decree that any particular person should go astray but stated that every one of those who did stray into idolatry would not have done so unless they wanted to. The Creator merely made known here the general behaviour of the world of mankind. This was like the saying, 'there will be among this people some righteous and some evil'. Hence the evildoer may not say that therefore he was destined for evil because God told Moses that there would be evildoers in Israel. This is also like the verse which says that 'the poor shall never cease out of the land' (Deuteronomy 15:11). So also with the Egyptians all of whom did evil to Israel, if they had not wanted to do harm they need not have done it and the choice was theirs. He did not make a decree about any individual man, but made known that in the end the seed of Abraham would be enslaved in a land not their own. We have already said that it is not within the capacity of man to understand how the Holy One — blessed be He! — knows about future happenings.

Chapter 7

1. Because every man has been given free will, as we have explained, he ought to pay attention to repentance, confess his transgressions in words and wash his hands clear of sin, in order that he may die a penitent and be worthy of life in the world to come.
2. A man ought always to think of himself as close to death lest when he dies, he might be found in his sin. For this reason he should turn from sin immediately. He ought not to say 'In my old age I shall repent', for he may die before he is old. Solomon in his wisdom said of such: 'Let thy garments be always white' (Ecclesiastes 9:8).

3. Do not say to yourself that repentance is only needed for sins that result in action, for example immorality, robbery and theft. Just as it is necessary to repent of these, so it is necessary to investigate evil thoughts which one possesses and to turn from anger, hatred, jealousy and sarcasm, and from pursuing money, and honour, food and the like. From all these it is necessary to turn in repentance. Indeed these transgressions are more difficult to uproot than those that involve action, and, when a man is fixed in them, it is indeed hard for him to separate himself from them as the verse says: 'Let the wicked forsake his way and the unrighteous man his thoughts' (Isaiah 55: 7).

4. Let not the penitent think that he is far removed from the state of the righteous on account of the iniquities and sins that he did. It is not so. For he is loved and desired by the Creator as if he had never sinned, and further he is well rewarded and the reward is great for he had indeed tasted sin and left it and controlled his desires. The sages said: 'In the place where the penitent stands the completely righteous cannot stand'. This means that penitents always stand above those who never sin because they have controlled their desires more than the righteous.

5. All the prophets insisted on the importance of repentance because Israel could not be redeemed except by repentance, and already the Torah promised that Israel would repent at the end of the exile and would be redeemed immediately, as the verse states: 'And it shall come to pass when all these things are come upon thee, ... thou shalt return unto the Lord thy God ... then the Lord thy God will turn thy captivity and have compassion upon thee' (Deuteronomy 30:1, 2, 3).

6. Great is the repentance which brings a man near the Divine Presence, as the verse says, 'O Israel, return unto the Lord thy God (Hosea 14:1), and further, 'Yet have ye not returned unto me' (Amos 4:6), and again, 'If thou wilt return, O Israel, saith the Lord, return unto Me' (Jeremiah 4:1). These mean that 'if you turn with repentance unto Me, you will cleave to Me'. Repentance brings one who is far away near. Yesterday he was hateful before the Most High, horrible, distant and abominable. Today he is loved, sought for, near and a friend. So you find that the language used by the Most High to isolate the sinner is used to bring near penitents, both individuals and peoples, as the verse says: 'It shall come to pass that instead of saying "Ye are not my

people" there will be said to them "Ye are the children of the Living God".' (Hosea 2:10). The verse said of the wickedness of Coniah: 'Write ye this man childless, a man that shall not prosper in his days' (Jeremiah 22:30), and 'though Coniah son of Jehoiakim king of Judah were the signet upon My right hand, yet would I pluck thee thence' (Jeremiah 22:24). But when he repented in exile it was said of his descendant Zerubbabel: 'In that day, saith the Lord of hosts, will I take thee, O Zerubbabel, my servant, the son of Shealtiel, saith the Lord, and will make thee as a signet' (Haggai 2:23).

7.   How excellent is the state of repentance? Yesterday the penitent was separated from the Lord God of Israel, as the verse states: 'But your iniquities have separated between you and your God ... that he will not hear' (Isaiah 59:2) and 'When ye make many prayers, I will not hear' (Isaiah 1:15). If he obeys commandments, they are thrown in his face, as the verse says: 'Who is there even among you that would shut the doors for nought?' (Malachi 1:10). Today he is close to the Divine Presence as the verse says: 'Ye that did cleave unto the Lord your God are alive ...' (Deuteronomy 4:4); and 'Before they call, I will answer and while they are yet speaking, I will hear' (Isaiah 65:24). He fulfils the commandments and accepts them with quietness and joy, as it is said: 'God now accepteth thy works' (Ecclesiastes 9:7) and longs for them. For the verse states: 'Then shall the offering of Judah and Jerusalem be pleasant unto the Lord, as in the days of old, and as in former years' (Malachi 3:4).

8.   The conduct of penitents is to be lowly and very modest. If fools reproach them for their past deeds and say 'yesterday you did so and so, yesterday you said so and so', they must not feel it but hear and be glad because that bestows merit on them. For as long as they are ashamed of their deeds and are disgraced by them, their virtues increase and they are raised up. It is a grievous sin to say to a penitent 'remember your former deeds' or to mention them before him to shame him, or to mention similar matters to remind him of what he had done. All that is forbidden. Warnings against 'damaging utterances' are included in the Torah when it cautions: 'Ye shall not therefore oppress one another' (with words) (Leviticus 25:17).

Chapter 8

1.   The hidden treasure for the righteous is the life in the world to come. This is the life in which there is no death and

where there is good but no evil, as the verse in the Torah states: 'that it may be well with thee, and that thou mayest prolong thy days' (Deuteronomy 22:7). In tradition we learn that it may be well with thee in a world entirely good and that thy days may be prolonged in a world which is limitless which is the world to come. The reward of the righteous is that they shall be worthy to enjoy this and live in its good. The retribution of the wicked is that they shall not be worthy of this life but they will be cut off and die. All who are not worthy of this life are as dead as those who never live. They are cut off by their evil and lost like animals. This cutting off is mentioned in the Torah which says, 'that soul shall utterly be cut off' (Numbers 15:31): according to tradition this means cut off from this world and surely also cut off from the world to come. That is to say that the spirit which separates from the body in this world will not be worthy of life in the world to come.

2.   In the world to come there is no body or substance but only the spirits of the righteous like the messengers of the Lord. Because there is no substance there is no eating or drinking and none of the other things which the bodies of human beings require in this world. No thing will befall which happened to the body in this world such as sitting and standing, sleeping, dying, grieving or laughing and such like. Thus the early sages said that in the world to come there is no eating, or drinking, or mating, but the righteous will sit with garlands on their heads and be delighted by the splendour of the Divine Presence. Thus it is made clear to you that there is no body, because there is no food or drink, and the words 'the righteous shall sit' are figurative and mean that the righteous will be without fatigue and weariness. In the same way when it says 'garlands on their heads' it means that they know they share in the life of the world to come and that they deserve it. This is the crown of which Solomon said 'the crown wherewith his mother crowned him' (Song of Songs 3:11), and again Isaiah 35:10 says 'everlasting joy upon their heads'. This pleasure is not something placed on the head. The sages spoke of that crown as understanding. What does 'being delighted by the Divine Presence' mean? It means that they will know and reach the truth of the Holy One — blessed be He! — in a way which they were not able to do in a dark and lowly body.

3.   The spirit as spoken of here is not the breath necessary for the body but the form of knowledge which comes from

the Creator according to the strength of the spirit and reaches out to thoughts on metaphysics. These are the matters which we have explained in the fourth chapter of the Treatise on the Fundamentals of the Torah, and spirit is used thus in the present context. In such existence there is no death because death only happens to a body. There are no bodies but what is termed the 'bundle of life', as the verse states: 'The soul of my lord shall be bound in the bundle of life' (1 Samuel 25:29). This is the greatest reward of all and good beyond which there is no better. It is what all the prophets longed for.

4.   This reward was spoken of figuratively by many names— the Mountain of the Lord, His Holy Place, the Holy Way, the Courts of the Lord, the Delight of the Lord, Tent of the Lord, Temple of the Lord, House of God, the Lord's Gate. The sages described this good metaphorically as the feast prepared for the righteous, but the general description was the world to come.

5.   There is no greater punishment than the cutting off of the spirit as unworthy of that life, even as the verse says, 'That soul shall be utterly cut off, his iniquity shall be upon him' (Numbers 15:31). This destruction is what the prophets called metaphorically the pit of destruction and the Valley of Hinnom, the inferno, the leech, each of these meaning end and obliteration. It is annihilation from which there is no regeneration, loss that is never regained.

6.   It may be that you will think lightly of this good. It may seem that there is no reward for observing the precepts and for the man who keeps wholly to the paths of truth, and that it is better to eat and drink well, enjoy lovely women, dress in embroidered garments of fine linen, and dwell in ivory tents and be served with vessels of silver and gold as the foolish, licentious, indulgent Arabs imagine. Scholars and the intelligent know that all these things are vain and futile, they are not profitable and no good comes from them in this world. Because we have bodies and forms, all these things are necessary, for the body needs them in order to exist and remain healthy, but the spirit has no longing or desire for them. When there is no body all these things are as nought. As for the great good which will come to the spirit in the world to come, there is no way in this world to reach out and understand that since we know only bodily good in this world and crave only for that good. But the great good of the hereafter cannot be compared with the good of this

world except by metaphors. Truly it is not possible to compare the good of the spirit in the world to come with the good of the body in this world from eating and drinking. Because the great good to come cannot be fathomed there is no way to make comparisons, as David said: 'O how great is Thy goodness, which Thou hast laid up for them that trust in Thee' (Psalm 31:19).

7.   How ardently David longed for the life of the world to come, as the verse says: 'I had fainted, unless I had believed to see the goodness of the Lord in the land of the living' (Psalm 27:13). Already the ancient sages made known to us that it is not within the capacity of man to apprehend' the good of the world to come clearly, or to know its grandeur, beauty and might. Only the Holy One — blessed be He! — knows that. All the benefits which the prophets prophesied about to Israel are bodily things which Israel might enjoy in the days of the Messiah when sovereignty would be restored to Israel. But with the good of the world to come there was no comparison or measure. The prophets did not describe it or lessen it by comparisons. This is what Isaiah said: 'Neither hath the eye seen, O God, beside Thee, what He hath prepared for him that waiteth for Him' (Isaiah 64:4), as if saying that the good which the prophets could not see, the Lord saw, and this is what He provides for the man who waits on Him. The sages said that all the prophets only prophesied about Messianic days and that the world to come is seen only by the Lord.

8.   Although the sages speak of the world to come, this does not mean that it is not present now or that the world will be destroyed and after that such a world would come. It is not so; it is accessible now and established, as the verse says: 'Thy goodness which Thou has laid up for them that fear Thee, which Thou has wrought for them that trust in Thee' (Psalm 31:19). They only called it the world to come to show that it comes to man after life in this world in which we exist with body and spirit.

Chapter 9

1.   Now that it is known that reward is given for observing the precepts and that the good things, of which we shall be worthy if we observe the way of the Lord, are written of in the Torah as the world to come, 'that it may be well with thee, and that thou mayest prolong thy days' (Deuteronomy

22:7). It is known that the punishment which is given to evildoers who desert the paths of justice is to be cut off and as the verse in the Torah states, 'that soul shall utterly be cut off; his iniquity shall be upon him' (Numbers 15:31). What then does the Torah say when it teaches 'If ye hearken this will happen to you and if you do not hearken this will befall you'. This refers to what happens in this world, for example, plenty and want, war and peace, independence and oppression, settlement and exile, good fortune in work or loss, and other sayings of the Covenant. All these benefits will follow when we observe the Torah's commands, and good things will come to us in this world. At the time when we transgress all the evils which are written of will befall us. However, these good things are not the end of the reward for observing the precepts and neither are the evils the end of the punishment for transgressing commands. All these matters are balanced. The Holy One — blessed be He! — gave us the Torah as a tree of life and he who performs what is written in it and understands its meaning entirely and correctly is worthy of life in the world to come. His worthiness depends on the magnitude of his actions and the amount of his wisdom. We are promised in the Torah that, if we obey with gladness and willingly and are guided always by its wisdom He will remove from us all the things which prevent us from observing it, such as sickness, war and famine and the like. He will shower on us all the good things which will strengthen our hands to perform the Torah, such as plenty, peace, increase of silver and gold, so that we shall not be busy all our days with the things which the body needs but may sit free to study wisdom to observe the precepts and so make ourselves worthy of the life in the world to come. Deuteronomy 6:24 to 25 states that if we observe all these commandments we shall be preserved in this world and have merit in the hereafter. He likewise made known to us in the Torah that if we desert the commands intentionally and busy ourselves with the futilities of the times, as is meant in the verse: 'Jeshurun waxed fat, and kicked' (Deuteronomy 32:15), then the Judge of Truth will remove from the deserters all the good of this world that has strengthened their hands to rebel and will bring upon them all the evil that has prevented them from earning the world to come in order to destroy them by their own evil. Thus it is written in the Torah: 'Because thou servedst not the Lord thy God with joyfulness and with gladness of heart, for the abundance of all things;

therefore shalt thou serve thine enemies which the Lord shall send against thee' (Deuteronomy 28:47,48). The explanations of the blessings and curses is thus interpreted. If you will serve the Lord in joy and observe His way, then all the blessings will be showered upon you and He will remove the curses from you until you will be free to study Torah and be busy with it so as to be worthy of the world to come. Then it may be well with you in a world which is entirely good, and your days prolonged in the world to come. You will find yourself worthy of two worlds, the good life in this world which leads you to the world to come. If one does not gain wisdom here and do good, how can one attain anything? The verse says: 'for there is no work, nor device, nor knowledge, nor wisdom, in the grave' (Ecclesiastes 9:10). If you forsake the Lord and follow eating and drinking and immorality and the like, He will bring upon you all the curses and remove all blessings until you end your days in alarm and terror and have no freedom or peace of body to observe the precepts. You will be excluded from life in the world to come and so have lost two worlds. For as long as a man is occupied in this world with sickness, war and famine, he cannot apply himself to wisdom or to the commandments which make one worthy of life in the world to come.

2.   Because of this all the prophets and sages of Israel longed for the days of the Messiah that they might be freed from governments which would not leave them to study the Torah, and perform commandments properly, and that they might have a quiet place to increase wisdom and become worthy of life in the world to come. For in those Messianic days intelligence, and wisdom and Truth would increase. The verse says, 'For the earth shall be full of the knowledge of the Lord, as the waters cover the sea' (Isaiah 11:9) and again, 'They shall teach no more every man his neighbour, and every man his brother, saying, Know the Lord: for they shall all know Me, from the least of them unto the greatest' (Jeremiah 31:34), and again, 'I will take away the stony heart out of your flesh' (Ezekiel 36:26). For the sovereign who will arise from the seed of David will be wiser than Solomon and have the gift of prophecy reaching to that of Moses our teacher. Therefore he will teach all the people and instruct them in the path of the Lord. And all the nations will come to listen as the verse say: 'And it shall come to pass in the last days, that the mountain of the Lord's house shall be established in the top of the mountains' (Isaiah 2:2). The

final reward and good which has neither interruption nor
diminution is the world to come. But in the days of the
Messiah in this world things will go on as usual, except that
Israel will have its own government. The ancients long ago
said that there would be no difference between the world
of today and the days of the Messiah except for the obliteration of oppressive governments.

Chapter 10

1.   No man may say, 'See, I observe the precepts of the
Torah and occupy myself with its wisdom in order to
receive all the blessings written therein, or to be worthy of
life in the world to come. I shall separate myself from the
transgressions which the Torah has warned us about so as to
be saved from the curses described in the Torah and that I
may not be cut off from life in the world to come. It is not
seemly to serve the Lord in that way. The servant who serves
thus does so from fear which is not the way of the prophets
and sages. The Lord is served thus only by the illiterate
or by women and children who have been trained to serve
Him out of fear until they have enough knowledge to serve
out of love.
2.   He who serves out of love occupies himself with the
Torah and the precepts and follows the paths of wisdom, not
for wordly benefit or for fear of evil, or to inherit good but
follows the Truth for its own sake, and in the end good
comes. This state of being is very high and not every wise
man can attain it. It was the state of Abraham our father
whom the Holy One — blessed be He! — called 'His beloved
one' because he only served out of love. This state is that
which the Holy One — blessed be He! — commanded us
through Moses saying 'And thou shalt love the Lord thy God'
(Deuteronomy 6:5).   When a man loves the 'Most High'
properly, he performs all the commandments in love.
3.   And what is this proper love? It is that he should love
the Lord so strongly that his spirit is bound to the love of
God and drawn to it always like a lovesick person, whose
mind is never free from the love of a certain woman and is
drawn to her always whether he is standing or sitting, eating
or drinking. More than this should be the love for the Lord
continually in the heart of those who love Him all the time,
even as we are commanded 'with all thy heart and all thy

spirit'. Solomon said of this figuratively, 'I am sick of love' (Song of Songs 2:5) and all the Song of Songs is an allegory of this matter.

4.   The sages of old said perhaps you will think 'I shall study Torah in order that I may become rich, or that I shall be called 'Rabbi' or to receive reward in the world to come'. The verse says: 'That thou mayest love the Lord thy God' (Deuteronomy 30:20) implying 'whatever you do, do it out of love'. Further the sages said, 'seek the commandments for their own sake not for reward'. The great sages advised the wisest of their pupils and especially the most intelligent, 'be not as servants who serve a master for reward but like servants who minister without reward', that is for love.

5.   Anyone who studies the Torah for gain or to prevent retribution coming upon him does not study it for its own sake. One who studies neither in fear nor for reward studies for love of the Lord of all the earth; he is the man who studies the book for its own sake. The sages said that man should always busy himself with the Torah even if not for its own sake because such study may develop into love. So if one is teaching women and children and the illiterate, it is well to teach them to serve in fear and in hope of reward, until their knowledge develops and they become wiser, and there is revealed to them slowly the secret. They then become accustomed to it gradually and understand and serve out of love.

6.   It is well known and quite clear that the love of the Holy One — blessed be He! — is not bound to a man's heart unless he feels it constantly and properly, and he deserts everything and leaves all else except the love of the Holy One even as He commanded saying 'with all thine heart, and with all thy soul' (Deuteronomy 6:5). No one loves the Holy One — blessed be He! — except by the experience of knowing Him, and according to that knowledge, whether little or much. So it is necessary for a man to dedicate himself to understand and discern, and by wisdom and insight to come to know his Master in so far as it is within man's ability to understand and to attain that love. This we have explained in the first treatise concerning the foundations of the Torah.

Here ends the treatise on Repentance.

RECENT PUBLICATIONS OF
THE ROYAL COLLEGE OF PHYSICIANS
OF EDINBURGH

47. *Symposium: Malignant Diseases:* including *The Biology of Carcinogenesis* by T. Symington (John Matheson Shaw Lecture 1974), *Immunotherapy of Cancer* by P K Bondy (Sydney Watson Smith Lecture 1974) and *The Care of the Patient with Progressive Cancer* by Cicely Saunders (Stanley Davidson Lecture, 1974). 145 pp. £3.50 (UK) £5.00 (Overseas).

48. *Symposium: Infections and Infestations:* including *Principles of Antibiotic Resistance* by Francis O'Grady and *Sexually Transmitted Diseases* by R D Catteral (Sydney Watson Smith Lectures, 1975) and *The Epidemiology of Respiratory Infections* by D D Reid (John Matheson Shaw Lecture, 1975). 124 pp. £3.50 (UK) £5.00 (Overseas).

49. *Symposium: The Eye in Medicine:* including *An Eye of the Physician* by E B Franch, *The Optic Nerve Head and Papilloedema* by J F Cullen, *'Twixt Cup and Lip'* by C I Phillips (Sydney Watson Smith Lectures 1976) and *A Medical Eye to the Ophthalmologist* by W S Foulds (John Matheson Shaw Lecture 1976). 108 pp. £3.50 (UK) £5.00 (Overseas).

50. *Symposium: Heritable Factors in Disease:* including *The Application of Genetic Principles to Prophylaxis* by Sir Cyril Clarke (John Matheson Shaw Lecture), *Hereditary Diseases of the Kidney* by M D Milne (The Davidson Lectureship), *Genetics and Cancer* by D G Harnden (Sir James D S Cameron Lecture) and *Inherited Causes of Mental Retardation* by J K Brown (Charles McNeil Lecture), 129 pp. £3.50 (UK) £5.00 (Overseas).

51. *Symposium: Prospects for Prevention:* including *Prevention of Obesity* by J F Munro (Sir James D S Cameron Lecture), *Prevention of Obesity* by J F Munro (Sir James D S Cameron Lecture), *Prevention of Smoking — Related Disease* by M A H Russell (Robert Phillip Lecture), and the *Prevention of Iatrogenic Disease* by Sir Eric Scowen (The Lilly Lecture) 127 pp. £3.50 (UK) £5.00 (Overseas).

52. *Symposium: Medicines from Prince Charles Edward to Prince Charles* by Ronald H. Girdwood (The Lilly Lecture). 20 pp. £2.00 (UK) £3.50 (Overseas).

53. *Symposium: Nutrition:* including *Nutrition in the Elderly* by A N Exton-Smith (Sir James D S Cameron Lecture), *Nutrition and Drugs* by J W T Dickerson (John Matheson Shaw Lecture, *Parenteral Nutrition* by H A Lee (Sydney Watson Smith Lecture) and *Myths about Nutrition* by Magnus Pyke (The Davidson Lectureship) 123 pp. £3.50 (UK) £5.00 (Overseas).

54. *Conference: Appropriate Care for the Elderly* ed. J M G Wilson *(The Problem; Possible Clinical Solutions, within the Community and in Hospital)* 104 pp. £2.50 (UK) £4.00 (Overseas).

The above are obtainable on application to the Librarian,
Royal College of Physicians, 9 Queen Street, Edinburgh EH2 1JQ.
(All prices include postage)